Hey Harvee. Sorry to interrupt your weekend but I just needed to tell you that I Just devoured your new book in one session! I'm all fired up! It's made me realise that my business is too focused on what was in it for me — not for my clients and for the broader world. I've referred back to the book all week — already integrating. Thankyou!

Bronwyn Candish,
Founder & Director of Cloudkeepers Chartered
Accountancy New Zealand.

HARVEE PENE

CO-FOUNDER OF INSPIRE - LIFE CHANGING ACCOUNTANTS

2 X 'TOP 100 COMPANIES IN AUSTRALIA'

STAND OUT

BECOME THE ACCOUNTING FIRM THAT PEOPLE WANT TO BUY FROM, WORK FOR & RAVE ABOUT

GREATER GOOD PUBLISHING CO.

A quick (and very important) word about integrity

You no doubt realise that the entire STANDOUT process is the result of investing many millions of dollars and thousands of hours of research and effort.

Clearly then, all the materials used in the STANDOUT book and STANDOUT resources are protected by copyright.

We could go through all the "legal-ese". We prefer to say that the content is protected even more by your integrity as a person.

To copy, give away or even lend the book (or parts of it) is not just illegal; it trivialises your own investment in it, and our relationship together.

Of course, special circumstances may arise where you want to copy parts of the programme. Integrity demands that you would ask us for our approval beforehand.

By going through this STANDOUT process & resources you expressly acknowledge and agree to that. You also expressly acknowledge that the STANDOUT material may not be shared in any way with anyone other than yourself.

Thankyou for your understanding and for your agreement.

Harvee@lifechanging.accountants

Copyright 2021

About the Author

Harvee Pene is the founder of Life Changing Accountants® and was recognised as 'One of Ten Outstanding Persons in Australia' 2019 when his then Accounting firm reached 10+ Million Days of access to food, water, health and sanitation given to families in need across 16 countries to help end poverty.

Life Changing Accountants globally are on a mission to give 1 Billion Days of Life Changing Help to families in need to help end poverty by 2030, by tipping 1% of their Time, Income or Profits, for Good.

He is best known for his children's story book about the UN Global Goals called **"ZERO POVERTY BY 2030"** which he wrote as a COVID lockdown project with his daughter Havana Pene (3) and were invited to speak about at TEDxYOUTH in 2022.

He is a testicular cancer survivor, the global face of men's health charity Movember and is studying to become a doctor.

CONTENTS

CHAPTER 1

Transition from Standard to Standout

How you too can transition from being a standard to a Stand Out accounting firm that your clients rave about and where your team members love working.

There are over 13,000 accountancy firms in Australia today, and if you're reading this book, you most likely own or work in one of them. And I hate to say it, but there's an overwhelming probability that your firm falls into that vast category I call "standard". For most of my decade or so in accountancy, there were probably four tiers of accounting firms:

Tier 1 — Big 4

Tier 2 — Larger firms outside Big 4

Tier 3 — Larger local/suburban accountants

Tier 4 — Local/suburban offices (smaller firms)

But these days, thanks to the great leveller we call COVID19, there are really only two types:

Stand Out

Standard

There are (sadly for them, happily for you) a great many more standard firms at work in Australia today than there are Stand Outs. I'd say that out of around the 13,000 firms plying our trade across the country, probably 12,900 of them are drowning in what I call the Sea of Sameness.

My objective in writing this book is to rescue you from that Sea, and help you turn yours into the Standout Firm that people want to buy from, work for and rave about.

I know about the sea of same-ness because I was once drowning in it.

See, I spent the last 5 years transforming a 'standard' accounting firm ('Inspire — Chartered Accountants') ...

... into a 'STANDOUT' accounting firm ('Inspire — Life Changing Accountants')

We became well-known for 2 specific things:

- For reaching $10M of proactive tax savings for our small business clients

- for giving 10 Million days of access to Food, Water, Health and Sanitation to families in need across 16 countries — a day of help given for every dollar saved.

As a result, we were twice recognised as one of the 'Top 100 Companies in Australia'. And as it's co-founder I was awarded One of Ten Outstanding Young Persons in Australia.

This book, however, is not a textbook. It's designed specifically to be an *experience-share* based on my journey. If you learn something that works for you, apply it. If what worked for me at Inspire doesn't resonate with you, don't use it.

To Stand Out, you have to Stand Up.

I warn you now — what I am advocating is not a path that you can simply pay lip service to and succeed. What this requires is a change in your philosophical attitude, and a move away from the traditional metrics you probably employ right now to assess your success.

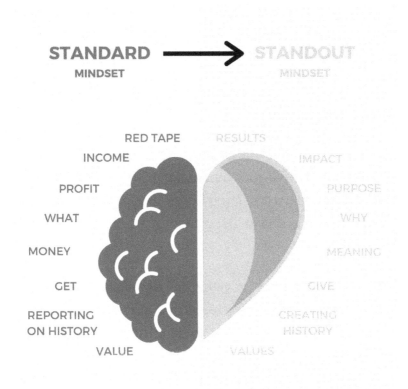

STANDARD ➡ STANDOUT
MINDSET   MINDSET

RED TAPE   RESULTS
INCOME   IMPACT
PROFIT   PURPOSE
WHAT   WHY
MONEY   MEANING
GET   GIVE
REPORTING   CREATING
ON HISTORY   HISTORY
VALUE   VALUES

No one is asking you to make this leap of consciousness on faith alone, that would be too much. Instead, I'll explain the logic and the benefits of the changes I'm recommending in detail and provide compelling evidence of how and why they work.

But you must understand, what makes every Stand Out business different from those still wallowing in the Sea of Sameness is that we've all made the commitment to Stand Up — to rethink our goals, our operating philosophy and our motivations.

What drives you?

The first secret is to understand what drives you and your business, and what that means for your capacity to Stand Out. You see, all of the firms I work with who have become Stand Outs share one thing: we all stand for something bigger than ourselves.

Let's go back to the question above: what drives you? If you're like almost every other firm in existence, the answer is simple: income. You strive to earn more revenue, and all your efforts are concentrated on that end. You're focusing on yourself, and whenever you do that the price of your inward focus is paid by your clients, your community and even our planet.

So I want you to stop that right now. I'm not asking you to become unreasonably altruistic or to sacrifice any part of your future — quite the opposite. I simply want you to focus on something bigger than yourself — and that something can be summed up in one word:

IMPACT

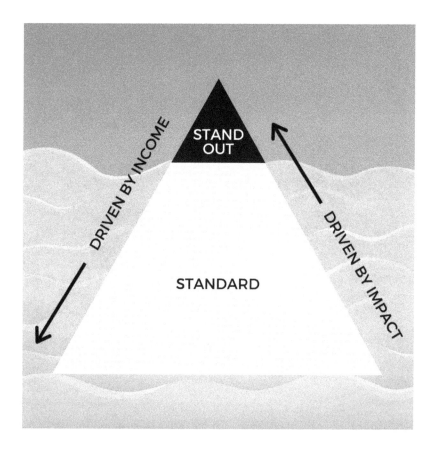

In blunt terms, if your driver is income, your tendency will be towards sameness, and you'll sink deeper into that sea we've already discussed.

But if your driver is the impact you make — on your clients, your team, your suburb, your state, your country and your planet — your performance will lift as you discover the rewards that approach brings, and you'll become a Stand Out.

Becoming well-known for the Results you create for your clients

Once you step away from the tired old driver of revenue, a whole new world opens up. The first thing you'll realise is that being revenue driven is so restrictive because it limits you to selling nothing but time.

The fact is, when you work that way, and you give your staff billing hours targets and you measure your success by that metric, you are giving away the thing that really counts in our business: *the value you provide to your clients.*

You'll never achieve Stand Out success by simply selling time and giving away ideas. But when you jettison that outmoded way of thinking, you'll realise that what your clients really want from you is your value — they want you to have a positive impact on their business and their lives.

And we can quantify that by assuming that what your clients really want from you is R.E.S.U.L.T.S. That is, they want you to commit to making an impact on their business through:

- Revenues

- Equity

- Surplus

- U.N. Global Goals

- Liabilities

- Tax

- Scaling Cashflow

Take David Patterson, who we helped transform from a partner at Silvan Ridge Business Advisers (read:

Standard) into the Stand Out position as 'The Bucket List Accountant'. Proudly he has 'front and centre' on his website (**www.thebucketlistaccountant.com.au**) ...

S is for Surplus Profits

$ 3,120,356

TOTAL INCREASE IN CLIENT PROFITS

U is for Contribution to UN Global Goals

3,120,356

TOTAL GIVING IMPACTS VIA B1G1 BUSINESS FOR GOOD

L is for Less Liabilities

$ 23,020,203

TOTAL REDUCTION IN CLIENT DEBT

When you commit to achieving all of these impact goals for your clients, you'll Stand Out from the sea of sameness. You'll Stand Out because of the results you create for your clients. And you'll enjoy the success that comes with that. In short, becoming the standout firm that people want to buy from, work for and rave about.

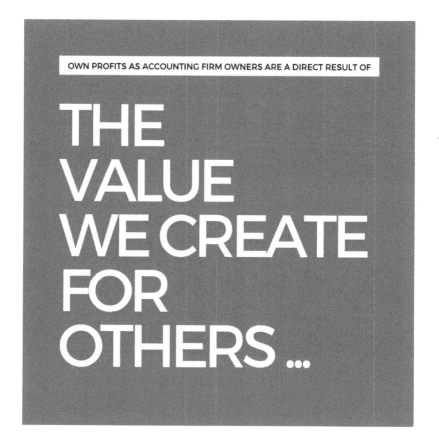

Not only that, through your commitment to the UN Goals for Sustainable Development, you'll be demonstrating your commitment to something bigger than all of us: the health of our Earth and the people who share it.

One crucial thing to remember here: if you have existing clients and you can't enrol them into your R.E.S.U.L.T.S./ Impact oriented philosophy, you probably need to reconsider your relationship with them.

14

The benefits of being a Stand Out.

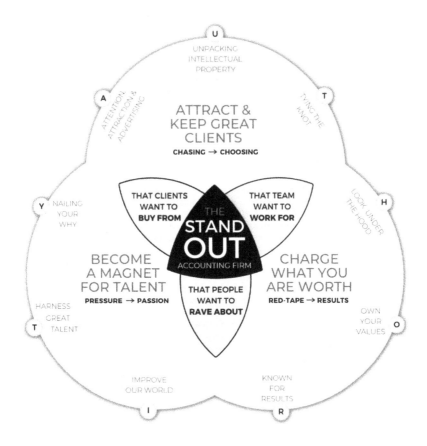

My experience in public practice and that of the global members of 'Life Changing Accountants' has proven time and time again that far from costing you, committing to making a bigger impact for your clients, the people you work with and the broader community, helps to enhance your business position.

In the main part of this book, I'll introduce you to the nine steps to going from Standard to Stand Out — an A.U.T.H.O.R.I.T.Y, creating a set of advantages that will elevate you from the Sea of Sameness by these significant indicators:

- You'll learn how to attract and keep great clients — people who want to buy from you because they share your attitudes, your goals and your philosophy. Here you can move from chasing your next client to selectively choosing who you work with.

- You'll discover what it takes to charge what you're worth (finally!) — as you move from clients who simply buy your time into people who are happy to pay you handsomely for the value you bring to their businesses. In other words, you move from Red-Tape to delivering Results. This will also turn them into promoters — people who'll rave about your business.

- I'll show you ways to delight your staff members as well as your clients, so that your business becomes a magnet for talent. By adding more people who can deliver greater value to your clients, your delight factor continues to grow. Here the realisation is that there's more motivation in measuring impact than there is in measuring time.

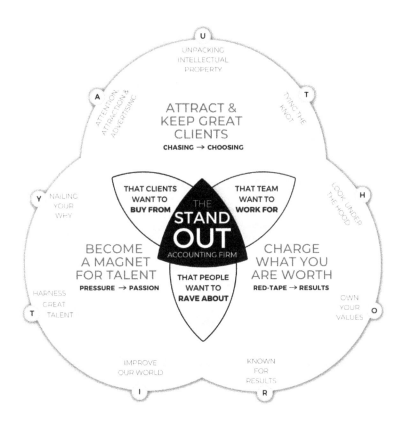

As you continue to read my ideas and engage with my story, you'll come to see that I'm very logical, methodical and meticulous. And with this book, I don't just have a structure: I've created a model where each of the benefits outlined above has its own set of chapters, each brimming with ideas and actions you can take. Let's take a look.

How we'll make it happen.

You'll see in this book there are nine key steps to lift your firm right out of the sea of same-ness and will help you be seen as an A.U.T.H.O.R.I.T.Y. where —

A is for Attention, Attraction and Advertising

U is for Unleash your Intellectual Property

T is for Tying the Knot

H is for Look under the Hood

O is for Own your Values

R is for Raising your Reputation through R.E.S.U.L.T.S.

I is for Improve our world

T is for the Talent you'll attract

Y is for Nailing your Why

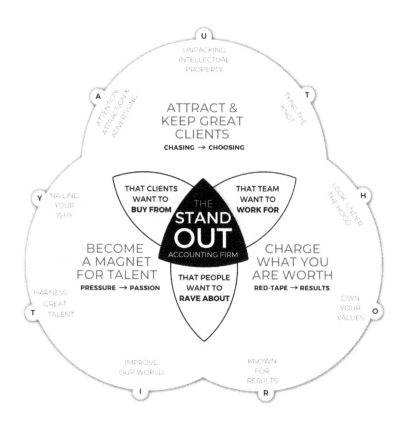

The nine-step A.U.T.H.O.R.I.T.Y. method comes with numerous ideas that have worked for me, and actions you can take to embrace the changes you'll need to make to become a Stand Out.

And while you're welcome to use these ideas, I encourage you to also use them as 'thought-starters'. That is, adopt the thinking behind each chapter, but create your own individualised approach to the practical application of those ideas. Remember, what you're doing here is formulating your own unique philosophy — based on the simple notion of delivering value across every facet of your business and personal life — so it's important that you make it your own.

See, I retired from 'INSPIRE' and started 'LIFE CHANGING ACCOUNTANTS' to pursue a much bigger (global) mission — to help Accountants Change Lives, Make an Impact and create a world where *every business is a force for good.*

That's why I wrote this book — to help you make more impact, influence and income than you've ever dreamed possible.

Read the story here, adopt the philosophy in your practice and enjoy creating a world-class culture and a life-changing business all because *Accountants Change Lives.*

Are you ready to Stand Out?

Let's go for it.

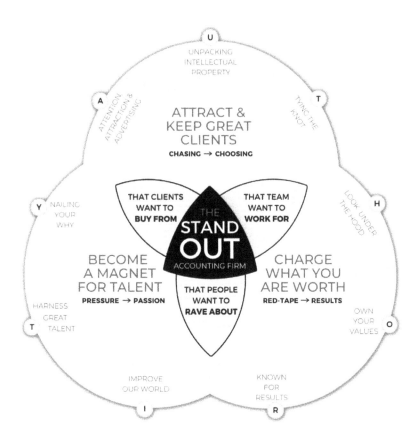

CHAPTER 2
A is for Attention, Attraction and Advertising

I love a chapter that starts with the letter A — it's so alphabetical. And as you can see from the title of this chapter, A stands for *Attention, Attraction* and *Advertising* which all mean kind of the same thing (but an attack of alliteration is always appealing).

In this chapter we'll look at ways of getting you noticed — not just in the "oh look, there's a dancing bear in a tutu" way, but in such a manner as to make sure that you're acknowledged, admired and applauded. Our aim here is to ensure that you are approved of, and subsequently approached.

We'll do that by showing you specific strategies across six 'SPEARS' that drive traffic to you and your business, bringing you qualified, buy-ready prospects:

Social media

Partnerships

Emails

Ads

Referrals

Speaking

THE SIX [S]PEARS — S is for Social Media

Why is that the first of my SPEARS? Because social media is the first thing many people turn to when they wake up in the morning. Or when they have a break, sit on a bus or even (so I'm told) when they go to the toilet.

Social media is ubiquitous, inescapable and can often be annoying. But in the right hands and with a finely honed strategy, it's an incredibly powerful tool. The fact that so many people misuse it is advantageous for people like us, who understand it and are ready to utilise it to its full potential. So let's dive in at the deep end.

Content is King

When you're using social media (our main tool is Facebook so I'll be referring to it throughout — but don't let that stop you from applying the same principles to Instagram, TikTok, Twitter or any of the other platforms in the long and growing list) what you post is incredibly important. The word I like to use here is *poignancy*, which my friend the Shorter Oxford English Dictionary tells me means "stimulating to the mind or feelings, delightfully piquant."

You need to construct or find content that is meaningful and impactful to the person watching. You need to engage their senses and their minds, entertain and enlighten them. Later in this chapter, under the heading *A is for Advertising*, I'll provide you with a 'funnel' strategy that focuses on content and how to make it work for you, and proves that in the fickle world of social media, content really is king.

Recency and Frequency

If content rules the realm of social media, the powers behind the throne are recency and frequency. It's a well-established fact that people are much more likely to buy from someone who's recently communicated with them. That, after all, is why those people with the golden arches and those other people who sell soft drinks in red cans spend billions of dollars globally every year to make their names as familiar as old friends (you knew exactly who I was talking about then, even though I didn't mention their names, right? Point proven).

So let's try a simple exercise: what did you last post about, and when was it? If the answer is that in 2018 you posted a video of yourself contentedly reading through *Schedule 7 — Tax table for unused leave payments on termination of employment*, that's a fail. In fact, if it's more than a couple of days or at most a week since you last posted, then it's a fail, almost regardless of the content. Post often, post intelligently and then post often again.

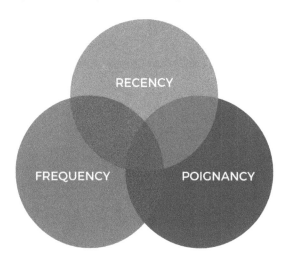

What are you going to say?

The content of course needs to be compelling, and video is a terrific tool for making hard-hitting posts. Take Karen Conlon, founding member of Life Changing Accountants, who isn't afraid to talk about her purpose, her goals for making an impact on her clients' businesses and the world at large, and her methodology.

As a result we've just ticked over 3,976,050 minutes viewed of the demand-generating videos that we've produced, posted and promoted for members of Life Changing Accountants globally — including for Karen — and from that audience, 10,061 high-quality leads have been generated, as at Aug 2021.

Here are some thought-starters for videos you could make, where you talk about:

- The key numbers that business owners need to know.

- Your philosophy on tax.

- The biggest impact you've ever made on a client.

- The most important lesson you've ever learned in business

- Your favourite tax saving strategy.

- Why you signed up for the UN Global Goals and which of the 17 mean the most to you.

"Great. And thank you," I hear you say but I'm also sensing that you may be thinking, "I need a bit of a push start. Is there an even easier way to get the content wheels turning?" The answer is yes. In short, you can start by simply reporting on the positive results you've been able to achieve for clients in say, the areas of:

- ✓ Tax savings e.g. "we just helped one of our clients save $xxxxx. They're going to re-invest that, spend it on a well-deserved holiday…

- ✓ Improving quality of lives. If you are contributing to efforts that provide positive impacts, what does that equate to? There's another piece of content.

✓ Inspiring them to achieve more in terms of raising their own profile. Personal appearances, talks, events. Caption a photo of you consulting, networking, sharing and (yup) share it.

Fun (and helpful) fact: If you do produce a video or have access to a video of you presenting, you can repurpose that using stills and captions. One of my videos was turned into 30 smaller snippets of powerful content and then subsequently 100s of photo/caption pieces of content.

Follow me on Instagram — @HarveePene

If you work with Life Changing Accountants, we help you make the signature videos you need, as well as providing more topic ideas. If you want to keep it in-house, you can of course have a company-wide brainstorming session where you create a list of social media post ideas, topics and approaches, and then implement them over the next six months or so — but you have to follow through.

We've done a lot of experimentation and we've made some interesting findings. Dry videos about business issues often didn't rate, but impact-related posts smashed it out of the park. Our story about our B Corp assessment got a lot of views.

To get maximum mileage, we sometimes put together a post featuring a quote from a person who's a centre of influence — Walt Disney, Nelson Mandela, Teddy Roosevelt, Richard

Branson to name a few — whose words reflect our own ideals. People love them!

Social media takes time though, and planning, thought and effort. If you can't put those factors in, hire someone who can or outsource – but don't fall into the trap of thinking that you can get by with the odd random post here and there. You need a strategy.

THE SIX S[P]EARS — P is for Partnerships

This particular SPEAR is all about forming mutually beneficial relationships with businesses and people who operate in the same space as you but are not in competition with you. What that does is allow you to access their clients and move in their sphere, learning more about your own target market and gaining valuable networking experience as you go.

So, how does it work?

Let's say your clients are predominantly small business owners 30 — 40 years of age. Or maybe you specialise in accountancy for medical practices, or law firms, veterinarians (see: www.aplaccountants.com.au) or online retailers.

The first thing you do is, you make a list of the people or businesses that your prime target also needs for their business. That could be marketing consultants, IT providers, real estate agents, brokers, financial planners, gym equipment providers, wholesalers, financiers and so on. The only criteria are that your prospect deals with these people, and they don't compete with you.

It's all about the quid pro quo.

Now you have your list, the question is, which of the names on the list will you approach? The answer is, the ones that you can create a *quid pro quo* situation with — because before anyone will enter into a partnership with you, there has to be a clear benefit for them. And there must be an advantage for you, too, hence quid pro quo (ok, that might do it for the Latin lesson).

Say your partner's client is getting financing for some new machinery or borrowing money to buy property, and there's a need for financial information. If the client's existing accountant is being slow or impeding progress it, your new partner recommends that their client talk to you.

The benefit to your partner is that he is able to process the transaction quickly and confidently because you've been over his client's financials. The benefit to you is that you're now in a position to develop the partner's client as your own. It's a Win/Win.

The quid doesn't necessarily have to be the same as the quo...

There are a lot of different ways you and your partners can help each other. If they have an email database, you can offer to send emails to your database on their behalf if they send emails on your behalf.

You can create social media posts that give your audience information about your partner's business, preferably with an offer, and they can do the same for you. It's a mechanism that allows you to post often and compellingly with provided content.

You can offer to speak at their events or appear on their web events, send gifts to each other's audiences — you send tax checklists and scorecards, they might send gift cards or vouchers for services. You can even offer straight out referral fees.

It doesn't matter whether or not both parties offer the same thing, as long as there's comparable value, and you each gain from the relationship.

As some inspiration, here's how I'd usually reach out to a partner 'cold':

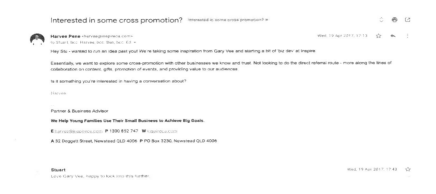

Here's another more common way I'd reach out to a partner, immediately after another successful engagement we've just had, while things are still 'warm':

Here's Yvette's response:

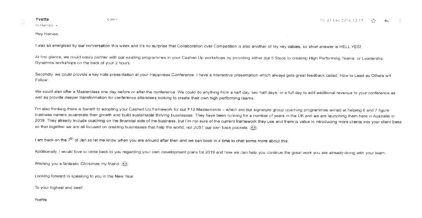

It's 'standard' practice for a partner of an accounting firm to spend 30 mins talking to a prospective client of the firm. As a founder of a 'Stand Out' practice, I'd much rather you spend the same 30 minutes talking to one partner who might introduce me to an audience of 100 x Ideal Prospective Clients. Get out there, meet the people your target market meets with every day and find ways you can help each other. It's really that simple.

p.s. drop us an email harvee@lifechanging.accountants if you'd like a copy of the Partnership Brochure that I'd send to give credibility to our win-win negotiations.

THE SIX SP[E]ARS — E is for Emails

Your email contacts list is a goldmine. Are you using it? Have you set up a proper database of your clients? You really ought to, you know. Platforms like Mailchimp can be set up for free in just a few minutes, so there's no excuse.

Communicating with your clients and prospects is easy with email. As long as you have their permission to send them emails, you can use email to invite people to live or online events, share interesting articles and inspiring snippets, and drop memes, photographs and videos.

K.I.S.S.

The key to success in this game is to keep it short and simple (that's my kinder, gentler version of K.I.S.S.). I work on the 'KISS email' principle — imagine you're writing an email to a mate for a barbecue at your place:

> *Paul, I'm having a few friends over for a barbecue this weekend — would you like to join us?*

It's easy, it's friendly, it doesn't need to be fancy or complicated, and it's designed to get a yes or no response. Now apply the same approach to a professional event, live or online:

> *Hi Paul, I'm getting a few local business owners/clients/*

37

entrepreneurs together for a web event/webinar/online meeting where we're going to brainstorm ideas to save tax / boost profits / protect assets / create wealth / become a business for good. Would you like to join us?

You can see that I've put in some alternatives for the type of attendee and the kind of event you'll be hosting, just to show that you can quickly and easily tailor it to meet the needs of your invitees.

A note on permission

To send emails like the ones we're discussing here, you need permission from the recipient. This can be implied permission — you are in regular contact with your clients and other contacts, so you have implied permission to send them emails on almost any subject. Just be sure you don't overdo it.

The other kind of permission is express permission — that is, if someone has responded to a Facebook post or contacted you via your website and has ticked the box for ongoing contact.

If you don't have either kind of permission, don't send these kinds of emails more than once or you could find future emails being sent straight to spam — your emails deserve better than that.

THE SIX SPE[A]RS — A is for Advertising

Advertising is about three important functions. Generating:

1. awareness of your brand,

2. familiarity with and an appetite for your offer, and

3. ultimately the motivation to engage with you

There are a million ways you can advertise, but most of them will be too expensive and too hit-and-miss for your purposes. You could spend $30,000 a week on television advertising, and you'll get a lot of people seeing your ads, but how many of them will be people you really want to attract to your business?

No, you don't need a scattergun approach, you need a sniper. And for that, we recommend online advertising — and even more tightly focused, social media. We've already covered that in some detail above, and in a minute, we'll look at an advertising specific strategy that has worked for us.

But first, the multi-million dollar question.

What are you advertising?

For your advertising to work, your brand has to be fully formed, and your offering must be compelling. Our points of difference are that we are Life Changing Accountants, and that we're committed to making an impact.

It's a strong position to occupy and I can highly recommend it, but again, it goes back to what I said at the start about your purpose and the kind of impacts you want to make. Remember though, advertising can be a two-edged sword and it will make a poor product fail faster — make sure you know what you're putting before the public, *before* you serve it up to them.

Now, how best to get that offer producing leads?

Welcome to the Funnel

This is a terrific Top-Middle-Bottom of Funnel strategy that we've used to build a highly-qualified audience of prospects before we go to the expense of advertising to them and creating a call to action.

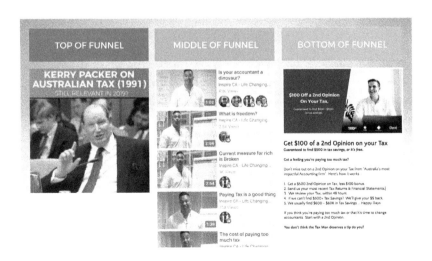

Top of Funnel

We start with a post that grabs the viewer's attention and holds it — this is the top of the funnel. The purpose here is purely to get the viewers' eyeballs onto the screen and keep them there. We once posted a short video of Kerry Packer talking about tax. He's direct, doesn't mince his words and most importantly, he was right on the money, and it strikes a chord with our audience. It can cost as little as $0.001 to get a viewer to watch a video on Facebook, so you can spend a little to get a lot of eyeballs — and our Packer clip packed such a punch we notched up many thousands of views.

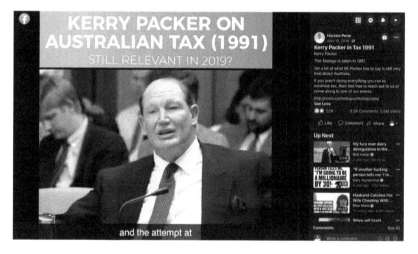

Middle of Funnel

Now when the potential client, who's excited at the idea of watching Kerry Packer lecturing politicians about tax, clicks on the video we've served up to their Facebook feed for less than pennies, they get a screen with a sidebar. On that sidebar we've used Facebook advertising to place a series of videos that we know will appeal to the kind of people who like what Kerry says about minimising tax. This middle of the funnel part, the sidebar ads, links to videos of me asking and answering questions like *Is your accountant a dinosaur?* or making bold statements like *Don't tip the ATO* and explaining *The cost of paying too much tax.*

Inspired by Kerry, the viewers of his clip often then click on one or more of our informative pieces and we're happy to give that information away for free. Because when we get their eyeballs, we also get their interest, perhaps their contacts and eventually their loyalty.

But how many eyeballs and more importantly, how many responses? Well, here's an example and I'm going to say that the response, for an accounting firm, was unprecedented. One post, millions of views, tens of thousands of shares and almost 5,000 comments. This demonstrated to us, and hopefully demonstrates to you, what can be achieved. An amazing experience.

Bottom of Funnel

And then, the knockout, or the bottom of the funnel — we serve them up with ads that make an offer, like getting a $100 discount on seeing us for a second opinion on their tax.

$100 Off a 2nd Opinion On Your Tax.
Guaranteed to find $600 - $60K+ in tax savings.

TED^x   nab   Dent

Get $100 of a 2nd Opinion on your Tax
Guaranteed to find $500 in tax savings, *or it's free.*

Got a feeling you're paying too much tax?

Don't miss out on a 2nd Opinion on your Tax from "Australia's most impactful Accounting firm". Here's how it works -

1. Get a $500 2nd Opinion on Tax, less $100 bonus.
2. Send us your most recent Tax Returns & Financial Statements.
3. We review your Tax, within 48 hours.
4. If we can't find $500+ Tax Savings? We'll give your $$ back.
5. We usually find $600 - $60K in Tax Savings ... Happy Days

If you think you're paying too much tax or that it's time to change accountants. Start with a 2nd Opinion.

You don't think the Tax Man deserves a tip do you?

We get a tremendous response on that strategy, because the people who are seeing the targeted ad have been reeled in by the engaging 'awareness only' clip of the great Mr Packer and have learned to trust us through our free informative videos. We've given them the poignancy, recency and frequency I talked about earlier. And by golly it works.

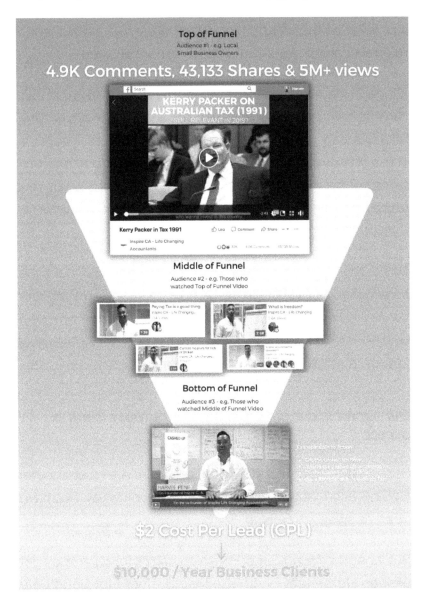

THE SIX SPEA[R]S — R is for Referrals

I think we can all agree though, that accountants probably will never be the world's biggest advertisers, so in our world referrals can be significant in gaining new business.

Although they're a touch random and unpredictable in that they can't be switched on and off like social media or advertising, referrals can generate well-qualified prospects. There's a sense of community and coherence that comes from someone recommending you to a friend, and the responsibility you feel to live up to that recommendation is an excellent motivator (as if you weren't already motivated enough).

This is the "rave about" part of the subtitle of this book, so here's a goal I want you to commit to: Transform all your clients into raving fans. If you turn a client, or even a prospect who's been referred to you, into a raving fan, every other goal in your business will flow on from that.

Our secret is our purpose, but our purpose is not a secret.

Back in the 'standard' day, we were a JAFA — just another flipping accountant — although the F word may not have been as sweet as *flipping*.

But when we found our purpose (to help Young Families get Cashed Up, so they could use their Business for Good!), we

45

created Life Changing Accountants and committed to things like the UN Global Goals for Sustainable Development and Buy One Give One (B1G1), we really started to take off.

Remember that a Stand Out firm is (irrespective of its size) an extraordinary firm that clients want to buy from, people want to work for and firms that people rave about.

An extraordinary firm that clients want to buy from, people want to work for and firms that people rave about.

Members of Life Changing Accountants globally are Impact-Driven. They are driven by and proud to share the positive impacts they create for their clients, their team members and their communities.

Additionally, they are STANDOUT firms because they stand for something bigger than themselves — Big Hairy Audacious Goals that reflect the positive impact they seek to make on our world.

So it all comes back to that pivotal issue of what you're going to stand for, doesn't it? And the wonderful thing is, when you commit to goals bigger than yourself, suddenly asking for a referral can become so much easier. You're not asking people to simply send business your way, you're asking them to participate in a worthwhile endeavour. I'll talk more about this shortly, but first some referral tips.

Here are those referral tips you ordered.

Let's say you have a client who loves your work but has not yet become a raving fan. Probably because you're an accountant, and you never thought that your relationship could be that gushy, so you haven't pushed for it. Asking such clients for a referral is still a good idea, but you have to make the request work for its bread. Here are a couple of ways we've put simple referral requests to work in the past:

I gave away 3 signed copies of my books at every client meeting, asking them *'do you know any business owners who might benefit from a copy of my Cashed Up book as a gift?'. We grew like wildfire.* This turned my client into the giver, which they loved, and then the receiver wanted to know more about us.

You don't have to actually write a book, although you know I strongly recommend it (and I can even help you do it, and you can contribute as much or as little as you like to the writing process). The point is, you need an asset that becomes the distribution method, and a book ticks a lot of boxes in the 7/4/11 touchpoints we'll cover in the next chapter, *U is for Unpack your IP.*

But sure, you can do it without a book — could be a gift card, another relevant book, a live or online event, a voucher for services, or whatever you think is appropriate.

The magic number method.

We're now at the point where we work on turning an ordinary prospect into a raving fan. Our method is simple, and it all hinges on our initial offering. This is our look under the hood, or second opinion on tax offer (see Chapter 5 — *H is for Look Under the Hood* for details). Because when we do our thing, we usually find a very, very magical number, and that is the tax savings the prospect could have made if we'd been their accountant.

We schedule a meeting with the prospect, which we call the delivery meeting, but before that we get them excited about the meeting by sending them a Magic Number message. That is, we tell them their magic number, and we ask for a referral:

Hi Tina,

I'm excited to tell you that we've found $43,520 in tax savings you could have made in our second opinion process. I'd love to tell you how we made those savings and how much we think you can claw back at our delivery meeting in a couple of days.

In the meantime, we're on a mission to find $1 million in tax savings for clients this year, and you can help us reach our goal. If there's anyone you know who could benefit from a second opinion on their tax, we'd love to give them a $100 Gift Card toward the process. And their tax savings will contribute to meeting our goal. It's a win/ win for everyone!

To refer us, please send your contact an email and CC us, introducing us. Mention the tax saving we've made for you if you like, and our goal for our mission. We'll do the rest.

Once again, congratulations on your awesome $43,520 in tax savings, I look forward to explaining more about it when we meet.

Can you see what we did there? We raised Tina's expectations for the meeting and gave her time to formulate the questions she'll need to ask ("WTF was my accountant doing?" "Is this legit?" "What will I do with the money?"). And when we asked for the referral, we invited her and her friend to contribute to meeting our Big Hairy Goal. We caught her at the moment of peak emotion and we asked her to join the cause.

Whether or not Tina provides a referral right there and then, we make the same offer at the beginning of our delivery meeting, and then again at the end. And if we give away three $100 discount vouchers, so much the better!

Cheers for our Cheerleaders.

The spectacular thing about the way our referral system operated was that there was no end to the growth it achieved. So much so we ran an epic one day workshop called *More Money Time and Happiness* — later renamed to WILDLY PROFITABLE — as a cheers to our cheerleaders for successfully referring someone from their network to become a client.

That monumental event was not only a lot of fun, it turned cheerleaders into raving fans, and they did whatever they could to be at the next event — it's a growth mechanism of stunning efficiency and success.

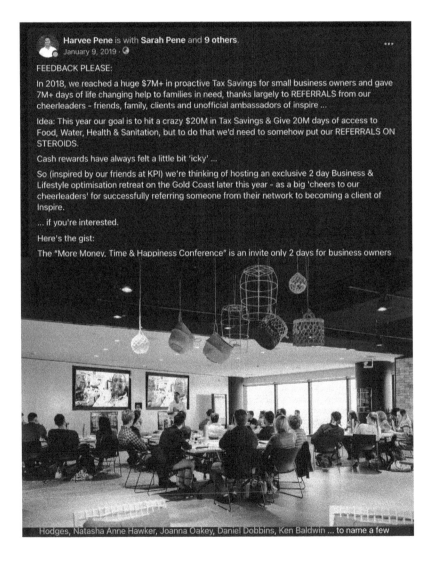

Harvee Pene is with **Sarah Pene** and **9 others**.
January 9, 2019 ·

FEEDBACK PLEASE:

In 2018, we reached a huge $7M+ in proactive Tax Savings for small business owners and gave 7M+ days of life changing help to families in need, thanks largely to REFERRALS from our cheerleaders - friends, family, clients and unofficial ambassadors of inspire ...

Idea: This year our goal is to hit a crazy $20M in Tax Savings & Give 20M days of access to Food, Water, Health & Sanitation, but to do that we'd need to somehow put our REFERRALS ON STEROIDS.

Cash rewards have always felt a little bit 'icky' ...

So (inspired by our friends at KPI) we're thinking of hosting an exclusive 2 day Business & Lifestyle optimisation retreat on the Gold Coast later this year - as a big 'cheers to our cheerleaders' for successfully referring someone from their network to becoming a client of Inspire.

... if you're interested.

Here's the gist:

The "More Money, Time & Happiness Conference" is an invite only 2 days for business owners

Hodges, Natasha Anne Hawker, Joanna Oakey, Daniel Dobbins, Ken Baldwin ... to name a few

As some inspiration, here are some photos of the 'WILDLY PROFITABLE' workshop that I ran as a reward for referrals 3 times a year in 3 capital cities across Australia:

THE SIX SPEAR[S] — S is for Speaking

S is also for self-evident. Because it's self-evident that speaking publicly and knowledgeably on your topic (which I assume is accountancy related) will enhance awareness of your practice, yourself and your offering, and drive traffic towards them.

Now, it's also true that statistically, fear of public speaking is more prevalent than fear of death — so, anecdotally, a large portion of the population would rather be in the casket than delivering the eulogy at a funeral.

But your fear of public speaking is something you must overcome to make this SPEAR work for you. I wasn't born a great speaker, but I knew the power of speech.

We worked on our signature presentations, and we got slowly better at speaking. The more we spoke, the more people we spoke to, the better we got and the more the audiences grew. And a great part of that comes from the fact that we didn't try and reinvent the wheel every time we spoke — we stuck to one topic we knew well, and we delivered it over and over again. But let me add that as far as you are concerned, as an expert in your field, there is already a treasure trove of topics in your own head — experiences, knowledge, stories, guidance — that people, potential clients are crying out for. Start with a topic or angle that you know very well and trust me, there are people out there that need to hear what you have to say on it.

Developing your signature presentation.

If you create and then deliver a signature presentation at every event you run or are invited to speak at (and that will happen — sometimes you'll even get paid), you'll do it so often it will roll off the tongue. You'll know the subject inside and out, you will have heard all the questions so you can't get thrown, and your confidence will soar.

So the question is, what topic would you choose to become your signature presentation? You need to choose it carefully, because you'll be living with it for a long time, and it needs to be something you're bloody good at.

My signature presentation on *Pulling more time, money and happiness from your business* was so successful and I became so good at it that when I decided to turn it into my first book (*Cashed Up*), writing it was a breeze.

So pick a topic that's dear to you, near to you and clear to you. It might be Profit and Cashflow, tax savings, making and taking more from life, or whatever. We spoke a lot about our purpose, and our work as Life Changing Accountants, and it really inspires and motivates people — and a lot of them are then keen to do business with us.

Okay, now is as good a time as any to spur you on by sharing my own speaker's kit with you. Have a look through the topics, the support material and imagine covering some of the same topics but using your own voice and point of view. I really want you to succeed at this so feel free to make this your guide.

SPEAKERS KIT | HARVEE PENE - Author of Cashed Up, TEDx Speaker & Co-Founder of Inspire - Life Changing Accountants

HAPPINESS IS THE NEW RICH.
INNER PEACE IS THE NEW SUCCESS.
HEALTH IS THE NEW WEALTH.
KINDNESS IS THE NEW COOL.
GOOD IS THE NEW GREAT.

Harvee Pene

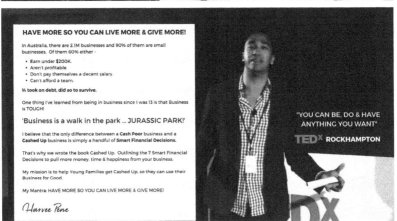

HAVE MORE SO YOU CAN LIVE MORE & GIVE MORE!

In Australia, there are 2.1M businesses and 90% of them are small businesses. Of them 60% either -

- Earn under $200K.
- Aren't profitable.
- Don't pay themselves a decent salary.
- Can't afford a team.

¾ took on debt, did so to survive.

One thing I've learned from being in business since I was 13 is that Business is TOUGH!

'Business is a walk in the park ... JURASSIC PARK!'

I believe that the only difference between a **Cash Poor** business and a **Cashed Up** business is simply a handful of **Smart Financial Decisions.**

That's why we wrote the book Cashed Up. Outlining the 7 Smart Financial Decisions to pull more money, time & happiness from your business.

My mission is to help Young Families get Cashed Up, so they can use their Business for Good.

My Mantra: HAVE MORE SO YOU CAN LIVE MORE & GIVE MORE!

Harvee Pene

"YOU CAN BE, DO & HAVE ANYTHING YOU WANT"

TED^X ROCKHAMPTON

HARVEE PENE

Author, TEDx Speaker & Co-Founder of Inspire - Life Changing Accountants.

ABOUT HARVEE PENE

Harvee Pene is co-founder of Inspire - Life Changing Accountants (Top 100 Companies in Australia - 2017 & 2018). He is a Business Advisor who helps Young Families get Cashed Up, so they can use their **Business for Good.**

With more than 20 years business experience, he is the best selling author of the books - **CASHED UP, LEGACY, 'BETTER BUSINESS BETTER LIFE, BETTER WORLD' & 'GOOD IS THE NEW GREAT'.**

Believing that Good is the New Great, his Top 100 Australian podcast "Inspiring Business for Good" showcases stories of Businesses that exist for the good of their Founders, their Team, their Clients & the World.

At 31 years old Harvee was blindsided by Testicular Cancer. He healed himself and is now a global ambassador for mens health with the MOVEMBER Foundation. Feeling like he now has a second chance in life, he tries to live true to his life's purpose - to **DO GOOD & INSPIRE OTHERS.**

As trusted advisor & accountants to the founders of Thankyou & ambassador for Buy One Give One and the UN Global Goals, Harvee is on a mission to see the

"Inspired by our friends (and personal accountants) from inspire. This is the most inspiring accounting firm you will come across. Their vision and execution is world class. Watch this space."

Daniel Flynn, Co-Founder & MD Thankyou

THE BOOK

Harvee launched his first book - co-authored with his best mate & business partner Ben Walker - in 2018 as a guide for business owners to pull **More Money, Time & Happiness from their Business.**

Harvee can include copies of the Cashed Up book as part of a speaking engagement package for your audience.

He can also arrange to be available for signing & photos after his talk.

CASHED UP

"If you're looking for ways to **Save Tax, Boost Profits & Accelerate your Cashflow,** then you definitely want to listen to Ben & Harvee!"
Glen Carlson, Co-Founder of Dent Global (Australia's 9th Fastest Growing Company)

59

THE TOP 100 PODCAST

Inspirational stories of businesses that exist for good - the good of their founders, their team, their clients and the world.

Harvee's goal is to deconstruct how business leaders make an impact and ultimately prove that **businesses who do good, do better.**

- Effective Giving and One for One.
- Business model design.
- Vision, Mission & Values led growth.
- Impact at scale.
- Revenue, Profit & Cashflow drivers.
- Attracting top talent.
- World class Leadership.
- And Leaving, Living and Leveraging a Legacy.

PJ Patterson on Leaving a Legacy & T
Inspiring Business for Good — 6 March

"Inspiring Business for Good is like sitting down & chatting with an amazing mentor over coffee each week. Harvee pulls out the gold from each person so that you can make the changes in your business "to inspire & do good." - **Emma Small**

AUDIENCES HARVEE HAS SPOKEN FOR

"Harvee. Thank you very much for your time yesterday. You definitely left an imprint on the team and the themes you spoke about were so aligned to our day and where the team was at it was perfect. You made an impression on my leadership team so have no doubt you can for the state and excited to have you be apart of the ANZ family."

Lara Thomas, District Manager ANZ

GOOD IS THE NEW GREAT!

SPEAKER TOPIC 1

Spectacular proof that - "BUSINESSES DO GOOD, DO BETTER."

In a world where 796 Million People find themselves living in extreme global poverty (on about $1.25 per day), who is best to solve this global issue? Politicians? Celebrities? Governments? Churches?

What if the solution were to come from Entrepreneurs, the natural problem solvers? And what if doing good for the world, was also good for you, your team & your clients too?

"Never has there been a more exciting time for all of us to explore this next great frontier where the boundaries between work and higher purpose are merging into one, **where doing good really is good for business."**
Sir Richard Branson, Virgin Group

STOP GIVING HALF YOUR PROFITS TO THE TAX MAN!

SPEAKER TOPIC 2

Think: Pauline Hanson. Barnaby Joyce. Senator Fraser Anning? When you think about these public servants, do you feel inspired to give them a tip?

It's impossible to get Cashed Up, if you're giving half your profits to the tax man!

So let's learn the strategies behind how we've been able to proactively save our small business clients $8M+ in tax & counting ...

"Epic Work! Trusts & Companies have been enigmatic to me for too long! The way you explained it, along with the common sense risk management is fantastic.!

Liz Kingston, Kingston Human Capital

BUILD YOUR PROFIT WAR CHEST

SPEAKER TOPIC 3

Ever noticed how no matter how much more you make, there never seems to be enough profit leftover?

Many growing businesses - regardless of size - suffer from a syndrome called "GROWING BROKE" where they find themselves making less and less profit on more and more income.

In a world where we tend to spend everything we earn, protecting your profit is vital.

You were put on this earth to do more than simply ... BREAK EVEN.

"Really great foundations to have a profitable business without sacrificing your passion."

Ale Wiecek, SQR One

GET **CASHED UP!**

SPEAKER TOPIC 4

Business in general is characterised by big winners and big loser but the majority of business owners exist between these two extremes, for better or worse.

Get Cashed Up is our guide to enabling business owners and their families to enjoy an extremely rewarding life, without living through uncomfortable extremes.

Jam packed full of strategies & exercises that work, case studies that explain and insights & stories that explain all the "HOW's" and importantly, the "WHY's".

If business is a game of numbers, it helps to know the numbers that count!

"Fantastic workshop! Very easy to understand and such valuable and insightful information. A must for every business owner!"

Airlie Coleman, Base Bookkeeping

KNOW YOUR NUMBERS

SPEAKER TOPIC 5

Imagine a small plane flying over the Pacific Ocean. Halfway across the captain announces, "I've got bad news and I've got good news."

The bad news is that the gauges aren't working. We are hopelessly lost, I have no idea how fast we are flying or in what direction, and I don't know how much fuel we have left.

The good news is that we are making great time!"

Does that sound at all familiar?

That's how most business owners run their numbers. They're flying blind with no dashboard to let them gauge where they are, where they are going, or if they are heading in the the right direction.

But somehow they always remain optimistic!

BECOME A GOAL DIGGER

SPEAKER TOPIC 6

Your complete guide to running a business that exists for Good. The good of its founders, its clients, its team & the world.

Learn how join the growing global 'Business for Good' movement by aligning your business to the 17 UN Global Goals - becoming a 'GOAL DIGGER'.

They are a New WAY & and New WHY for business owners to both grow their business, their impact and their legacy.

Welcome to a new pathway for business - or maybe even a new pathway for humanity.

"We can't be the experts on everything but knowledge is powerful so listen to these guys (Ben & Harvee)"

Dr William Huynh, Be Well Dental

INSPIRE BEFORE YOU EXPIRE
SPEAKER TOPIC 7

They say, "the two most important days of your life are the day you are born, and the day you find out why". So what is your purpose?

See, our days are numbered ... We don't know when our time on this planet will be up.

What if, instead of leaving a legacy, we could LIVE our legacy now.

Learn the why, what & how of living a life on purpose, enabling you to INSPIRE BEFORE YOU EXPIRE.

Harvee Pene from Inspire CA - Life Changing Accountants. Thanks for empowering our kids & inspiring our young change makers at Business Camp in Brisbane. We all LOVE our Cashed Up Clap!

Taj Pabari, Young Australian of the Year

ACCOUNTANTS CHANGE LIVES!
SPEAKER TOPIC 8

Most business owners think that "ACCOUNTANTS ARE BORING."

Truth is, they have the power to help -

* Avoid cash flow crises
* Protect family assets
* Eliminate unnecessary business expenses
* Grow businesses by focusing on KPI's
* Get clarity and a sense of control & direction
* Think through a business model & direction
* Ensure a legacy through Estate Planning
* Ask the hard questions
* Automate invoicing processes.

In short, Accountants Change Lives.

This presentation suits conferences, lecture halls & events of Accounting Professionals, Accountants & Future Accountants.

GET PROFIT
8 HR PROFIT ACCELERATION WORKSHOP

You were put on this earth to do more than simply ... BREAK EVEN.

But if you want to make more profit and less loss, you need to -

1 - Build a Profit War Chest.
2 - Know Your Numbers.
3 - Stop Giving Half Your Profits to the Tax Man.

Enjoy an inspiring day of mastering the 5 P's of Profit - Psychology, Priority, Predictability, Protections & Purpose.

"What a magic day with Harvee and Ben at Get Profit ♥. The key framework these guys provide has been a missing piece in my business operations. Super grateful to come away with so much clarity for how to get cashed up so my business can do more good in the world. 2"

Jaemin Frazer, The Insecurity Project

MORE MONEY, TIME & HAPPINESS

2 DAY BUSINESS & LIFESTYLE OPTIMISATION RETREAT

Over two days you will develop a series of 12 month plans, strategies and budgets to help you pull more money, time and happiness from your business.

These will become valuable assets that you will refer to on a daily or weekly basis to allow you to Boost Profits and Accelerate Cashflow in your business.

Based on implementation of the model in the Cashed Up book - 7 steps to pull more money, time & happiness from your business.

"I've never met such groovy, amazing and connected Accountants in my life!"

Phillip Di Bella, The original King of Coffee Culture

WEALTH FOR GOOD

2 DAY PERSONAL WEALTH & LIFESTYLE RETREAT

Let's turn your business profits into personal assets that will build your family legacy.

Most arguments in a marriage are around Money, and our mission is to reverse the statistics on divorce by getting couples on the same page about finances.

Focused around building true riches in all areas of wealth - Financial, Time, Physical & Relationships.

"Inspire CA takes the fear away from numbers and makes it real. They feel more like a business partner than just an Accountant."

Sharon Cliffe, Cider Consulting

BUSINESS FOR GOOD

2 DAY PURPOSE, PROFIT & PHILANTHROPY RETREAT

You've probably heard the adage - Businesses who do good, do better. Well this retreat will help you do better at doing good.

Over 1.5 inspiring days we will re-engineer your business to make super profits. This will be followed by a life-changing visit to a village to see first hand the impact that can be made when a business choses to use their profits for a higher purpose.

This is an international retreat hosted annually from 2020 in Bali, Vietnam & Cambodia.

"It's great to learn more about the bigger impact so many businesses are making thanks to the business for good movement. Every conversation has been incredibly inspiring."

Brandon Peart, Content Jet

ACCOUNTANTS FOR GOOD

2 DAY PURPOSE, PROFIT & PHILANTHROPY RETREAT
for Accounting Firm Owners.

How can Accountants go from 'Boring' to 'Great' by doing more GOOD?

The UN Global Goals provides a NEW WAY & a NEW WHY for the Accounting Profession to grow their business and the impact they have on the world.

This retreat suits Accounting firm owners and will be run regularly in USA, UK & AU from 2020.

"Harvee shows a real generosity of spirit when sharing his time and he is truly insightful and knowledgeable in the areas of business improvement for today's professional practice."

Chris Beks, Ceebeks Accountants & Advisors

Topic 1
GOOD IS THE NEW GREAT!

Topic 2
STOP **GIVING HALF YOUR PROFITS TO THE TAX MAN!**

Topic 3
BUILD YOUR **PROFIT WAR CHEST**

Topic 4
GET **CASHED UP!**

Topic 5
KNOW **YOUR NUMBERS**

Topic 6
BECOME A **GOAL DIGGER**

Topic 7
INSPIRE **BEFORE YOU EXPIRE**

Topic 8
ACCOUNTANTS CHANGE LIVES.

Workshop 1
GET PROFIT
8 HR Profit Workshop

Retreat 1
MORE MONEY, TIME & HAPPINESS
2 Day Business Profit & Lifestyle Retreat.

Retreat 2
WEALTH FOR GOOD
2 Day Personal Wealth & Lifestyle Retreat

Retreat 3
BUSINESS FOR GOOD
2 Day Profit, Purpose & Philanthropy Retreat for Business Owners.

Retreat 4
ACCOUNTANTS FOR GOOD
2 Day Profit, Purpose & Philanthropy Retreat for Accounting Firm Owners.

Harvee's Speaker Topic Summary - Inspiring Keynotes, Panel Discussions, Workshops & Retreats

LET'S TALK!

Harvee will do everything it takes to make sure your event is a huge success. To enquire about Harvee's speaker fee and to make a booking please contact Sarah Pene.

Speaker Enquiries to Sarah Pene harvee@harveepene.com

65

So even if you're terrified, get started. Schedule events — include other speakers if you must — and make them regular. Pick your signature topic and develop a convincing presentation around it. The more you speak, the more you'll enjoy speaking, and the more people will come to hear what you have to say.

As some inspiration, here's a typical 'pitch' to speak at an upcoming small business event that would usually fetch a speaker fee of between $3,000 and $6,000 (when in reality I should have been paying them for putting me in front of 50 to 100 prospective business clients):

Sharpen your SPEARS

As you may know, the primary growth factor in a rainforest is the sun. The more sun a tree receives, the faster it will grow. As the tree grows it then gets more sun, so it grows taller still.

In short: you're either a tall tree in the sun or a small shrub stuck in the dark. And there's not a lot in between.

Same too for Accounting firms — you're either STANDARD or STANDOUT.

This chapter, long as it is, is just a taster of what the SPEARS method can do for you to get the attention (and then the leads) that you deserve.

So build your own quiver of spears, sharpen them, pick your targets and aim for the bullseye every time. You know I have faith in you, so go for it.

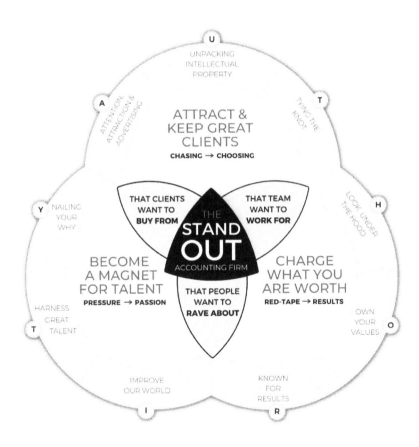

CHAPTER 3
U is for Unleash your Intellectual Property

Right now, you have the intellectual property, the talent and the wherewithal in your office to be well-known, in-demand and successful. All you have to do is find it, package it, present it and watch the accolades flow (along with the business and the profits).

My story is instructive.

How do I know that? A number of years ago, I was a partner in an ordinary suburban practice with a bunch of good clients but no real prospects for growth or change, perhaps a bit like you are now.

I knew I needed to do something different, and what that became was my commitment to making an impact, not just on our business but every business we touched, and on the world at large.

STANDARD STANDOUT

**INSPIRE
CHARTERED
ACCOUNTANTS**

INSPIRE
LIFE CHANGING
ACCOUNTANTS

When I first bought the firm I rebranded it from its 'standard' name INSPIRE CHARTERED ACCOUNTANTS to a more 'stand out' name being 'INSPIRE LIFE CHANGING ACCOUNTANTS.

I then architected the giving initiative 'Day for Dollar' and made a commitment that for every dollar we saved a client in tax, we'd give a day of access to food, water, health or sanitation to a family in need.

Putting it on the road.

From there I started taking potential clients out for coffees and lunches, wining and dining them to tell our story of impact and positive action, and hopefully convince them to change accountants. I'd stack five meetings a day, sometimes seven, and inevitably cover the $10 — $100 food / drinks bill.

And I grew the business exponentially (as well as my waistline!) through the pure grit and hustle of what I call 'Partner Power'.

Eventually I hired a business development manager who could consume the calories and tell the impact story to potential clients for me, and that worked for a while, but he moved on.

And I just couldn't go back to the same expensive, tiring, fattening process myself.

I built an asset.

So, I decided to build an asset — to find a way to replicate the same stories, sales strategies and ideas that we were giving away in our coffee chats and lunches. I developed a signature presentation on *7 steps to pulling more money time and happiness from your business* based on all those conversations. And then I had an epiphany.

I needed to change my ratio.

Changing my ratio

Here's the way I saw it. Before we changed our brand to one of impact, our contact ratio was usually 1:0. That is, we had the potential to make a difference, but we weren't getting an audience. With my endless lunches and coffee chats, I changed the ratio to 1:1 — I was dealing one to one with prospects. But it was consuming a lot of time and money, and not doing much for my health.

What if I could change up to a "1:Many" ratio? Speak at events, host events myself and begin to expound my ideas to a lot of people at the same time. So that's what I did. After all, I had my signature presentation, I just needed to widen the audience.

And that worked, but the bummer was, it still relied on me being there, giving out the same spiel and pressing the flesh. Although it was wildly successful, I was still looking for a way to improve the efficiency of it all.

Moving to the "0:Many" ratio.

The next step was to develop our social media activity — videos that sat on the web and let people come to my ideas instead of taking them to the audience myself, blogs, white papers and more to change the ratio to a very satisfying 0:Many. My ideas were reaching an audience and claiming real estate in their heads without me even being there.

And yet I still wanted an asset that would be a multiplier — I wanted to exponentially increase the Many in "0:Many".

And that's when I wrote a book.

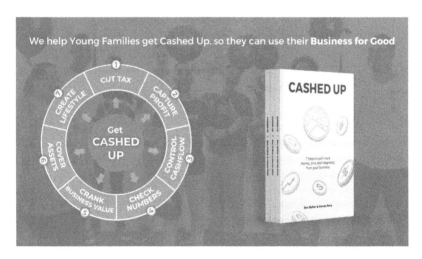

All the valuable intellectual property I'd developed in my meetings, my signature presentation, my online presence, meetings and events was still mostly locked away in my head, and I needed to get it out.

So I wrote a book called Cashed up — *7 steps to pulling more money, time and happiness from your business,* based on my signature presentation. The effect was immediate and electrifying. I gave away hundreds of books, to clients, prospects, event attendees and more. And then I sold even more — 10,000 or more in total. So suddenly my ideas were being delivered to a vast audience without me having to do anything but sign a few books and smile.

I'd learned the lesson that I'm giving you now — if you package up and present your IP, you're reaching thousands of people even when you're at home spending time with your kids.

Not only that, your printed words have a power and gravitas, as well as a reach, that can't be replicated any other way. Your ideas gain a permanence and presence that makes people sit up and listen. And if in your book you assert your commitment to making an impact, there's a credibility that can't be denied, and demands that you're as good as your word.

Don't just take it from me. Ask Jamie Oliver, who was just another brash young chef when he decided to put out a book. Or Scott Pape, who was a mortgage-broking farmer until he became the *Barefoot Investor*. And until he wrote a book, people used to say, "who the hell is Jason Cunningham?"

The impact just keeps growing.

The result of that first book was that we were able to make good on our promise to have a genuine impact. We stopped charging by the hour and started charging for the value we provided — our clients were happy to pay for our intellectual property, because they'd seen it in action and they knew that we were damn good at what we do.

This in turn helped us reach a massive $10 million of proactive tax savings for our small business clients, and that allowed us to give 10 million days of access to food, water, health and sanitation to families in need across 16 countries — a day of help given for every dollar saved. Our impact was and is real, palpable and documented.

I also started getting invited to speak all over the country — often paid appearances — and met thousands more potential clients along the way. And of course, I sold more and more books.

Taking the next step.

Since then, I've written and co-written quite a few books, each based on a simple, easily followed but insightful and practical methodology to achieve a particular objective. Any accountant could probably teach their clients ways to save tax, get cashed up or boost profits, but only we have packaged those ideas and that IP into handy books that can be read on a flight from Sydney to Perth.

Perhaps more importantly (for you), in writing all these books I've developed a formula that makes it easier and more effective to distil your intellectual property into a saleable commodity.

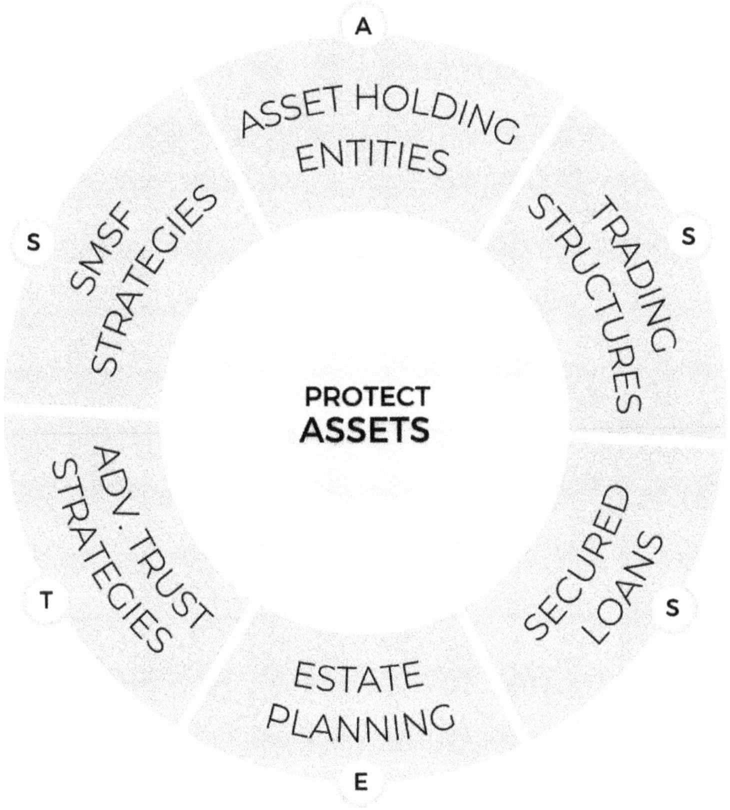

PROTECT ASSETS

- A — ASSET HOLDING ENTITIES
- S — TRADING STRUCTURES
- S — SECURED LOANS
- E — ESTATE PLANNING
- T — ADV. TRUST STRATEGIES
- S — SMSF STRATEGIES

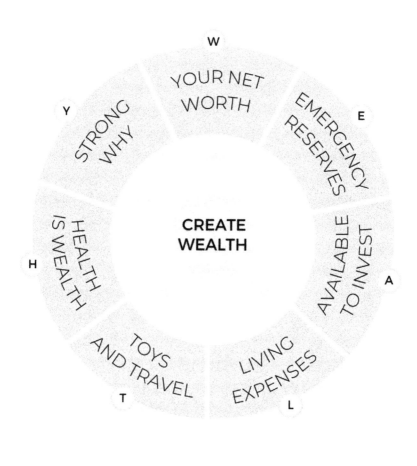

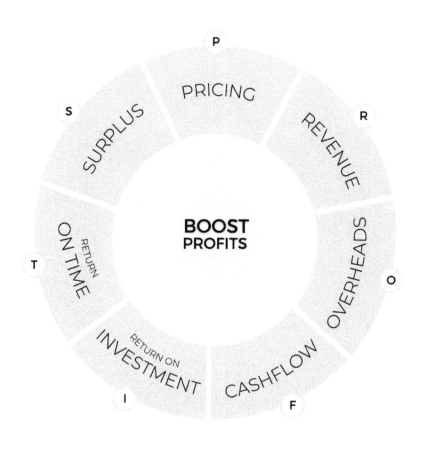

The 'how to' guide.

I know what you're thinking, "trust an accountant to make a formula out of book writing!" But this approach has worked for me time and time again, and I know it will work for you if you show a little discipline and inventiveness.

Now, writing books didn't come naturally to me, and my first book nearly killed me. But I learned to break what seemed like an insurmountable task into manageable bits — chapter by chapter and idea by idea — and I got through it. The problem was nowhere near as difficult once I broke it down to bite-sized chunks of work I knew I could do.

Here's how it works:

✓ 1 Book = 30,000 words.

✓ 30,000 / 10 Chapters = 3,000 words per chapter.

✓ 10 Chapters = Introduction + 7 Step Method + Bonus Chapter + Conclusion.

✓ If each Chapter = Just 5 key ideas.

✓ And if 1 key idea = 600 words.

✓ I just need 50 key ideas = 1 book.

Here's what my *10 Chapters x 5 Ideas x 600 Words Book Plan* looks like when mapped out on the wall.

It took a long time but eventually (with the help of my editor) I finished that book, and I realised that my method has legs. If I could break my ideas down to bite sized chunks and arrange them into a memorable and easily searchable format based on a word (like A.U.T.H.O.R.I.T.Y. or T.A.X.E.S.) or a concept (like CPR), I could write books on anything. And if I can do it, you can do it too.

And if you need help, talk to me. I'm always looking for co-authors, and I'll coach you through the process and show you exactly how it works.

P.S. Here are 5 more rapid fire tips:

1. Co-Author = Half the work + double the leverage. When you have a co-author, the formula (and the hard work!) is divided by two. Plus, once it's published you have double the leverage — as two people are promoting it, not one.

2. Mock Book. Get your cover printed and stick it onto another book of the same size. It makes it real for your team, family, clients, prospects, partners and most importantly, for yourself. I pulled off a major partnership deal with the Commonwealth Bank of Australia to host a book launch and a series of business builder events, with a mock book!

3. Don't bother running your own book launch event. Save the money to buy more books. Find an event or conference that is full of your target market and launch it there. I'm launching my book *Good is the New Great* at the B1G1 Business for Good Conference where I am a speaker. You'll probably be exhausted (and broke!) after doing your first book (I know I was!), so instead of putting together a big launch event yourself, tack on to someone else's.

4. Pay a bit extra to get your editor to contribute to the writing. If you're good at the first 80%, pay a bit extra to your editor to do the remaining 20%. We sat on our 80%

complete transcript for months and months until we decided to get our editor help sharpen everything up and take 20,000ish words written by accountants and make it 30,000ish words written by a professional author.

See you at the bookstore.

The key to all this is that the intellectual property you need to unleash already exists. It's in your head. All you have to do is organise it, package it and give it out to the world.

As long as it stays locked in your head, it has the potential to make a positive impact on your clients' businesses — but think of all the people who're missing out on your wisdom and experience. And all the people who could benefit from the wider impact if you commit to being a business for good.

Unleashing your IP is a matter of making the most of what's already there, and it will be the beginning of your journey to expanding your impact in ways you can't even begin to imagine now. Go on, you're ready.

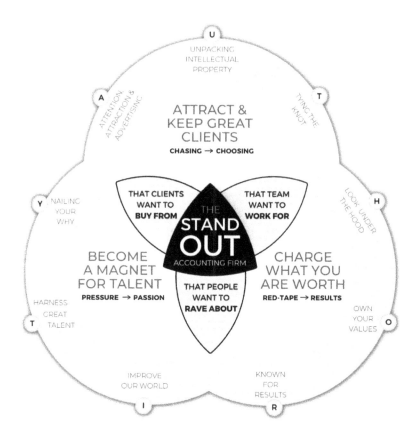

CHAPTER 4
T is for Tying the Knot

This chapter is all about how to get clients. "But surely," I can hear you saying, "this whole book is about how I get clients." To which I respond, no, this book is about how you transform your practice into a Stand Out practice, how you change your outlook to one of impact and purpose, and how you grow your practice through that change.

But this chapter is also about the mechanics of getting a client. The process that you need to understand and exploit if you're to grow your business.

Let's look at it another way.

Here's a thought you might relate to well: sales and marketing is a lot like dating and marriage (or "tying the knot" as they say). When we're out there marketing for new prospective clients, we're signalling that we're available, that we're attractive (well at least we think we are) and that we can be a great partner.

It's a great metaphor because it can dramatically shift your viewpoints and those of your prospects. For a while there, we had quite a lot of team members who were uncomfortable with sales, and so many prospects who hated to be sold to (but loved to buy!) that one day we decided to couch the entire sales process in terms of dating, which everyone can understand. And it worked wonders ...

The simple analogy lightened up the mood when it came to talking about sales. And significantly, we saw that it was true for both the team and the prospective client.

It gave much needed structure to the sales process, and as we've observed before, structure makes such a difference to everything you do.

So let's examine it in some detail now.

The first date.

On our first date, when we're courting a prospective partner we're scanning to see if we have common interests, common values and shared philosophies. Both sides are looking for signs of attraction in the other, and if they find them, the magic can happen. That's why it's crucial to showcase your values, your philosophies, your methodology and of course your existing happy customers.

In this context, it's your books, workshops, scorecards, podcasts, blogs, webinars and videos that are the vital first date a prospective client has with you. Do you currently have seven hours' worth of valuable content that prospective clients can consume (read, watch, listen to or do), preferably in a digital or scalable format? If not, do you have a plan to get those things that will make your first date a success? You'll never get to the second date if you don't.

That's why in reference to the first date in our very human sales process I would say -

> First Date — Learn about the 7 Smart Financial Decisions of a Cashed Up Business with the Cashed Up Book, Workshop and Scorecard.

Let's keep the sequence going. Let's go to …..

The second date.

Second dates in the real world are a good sign that there's some initial chemistry. You might say to yourself, *I've met someone and so far, I like what I see.* And you decide to go on another date to get more detail — to check out if this person might be 'the one'.

In a sales context it looked like this: we'd finish running the *Cashed Up* Workshop, I'd openly ask prospects in the room "If changing accountants was like going on a date, we've just come to the end of our first date together. How was it?"

Around a room of 20 or 30 business owners, we'd get things like "great", "loved it", "I want more," and some would even joke "I enjoyed myself but you're not getting a kiss!", which I can tell you, I, and my wife, were happy to hear.

So the invitation to go on another date was simply to take the next step which I positioned this way -

> Second Date — Let's take the next step by doing a Look Under the Hood, a $500 2nd Opinion on Tax, guaranteed to find you $500 in tax savings or it's free.

Check out the next chapter, *H is for Look Under the Hood* for more detail on the second opinion process.

Now, you have to know that when we go on a second date where we promise to find a minimum of $500 in tax savings, we always smash it out of the park.

In fact, a few days after the date, we send a message telling the client their *Magic Number*, which is the actual tax savings we've found (which makes the $500 minimum look positively paltry — we've found up to $70,000 in tax savings) — and invite them on the third date, the Delivery Meeting. The *Magic Number* message is a no-brainer guarantee that they'll be ready for the third date.

So now, we're ready for this ....

The third date.

On this important third date, things start to get a bit more serious and it's time to pull out all the stops. By now the prospective client has read the books, attended the workshops, become familiar with your values, philosophies and ideas and has even spent some money and time with your team one on one.

At the Delivery Meeting we answer all the client's questions around the tax savings we've found, and we present them with some urgent needs that need to be dealt with — an opportunity to go on a fourth date.

Given that we've just explained how we found them potentially thousands in tax savings, most clients jump at this chance.

Practically speaking here we might be doing a small project like - setting up Xero, amending tax returns, catch up on tax, new business structures etc — and was worded this way -

> Let's complete an 'Urgent Need' project upfront to help claw back $$$'s in overpaid tax, get up to date with the tax office and/or set up new business structures to help save tax and protect assets.

Then, not surprisingly perhaps, it's time for this ....

The fourth date.

This fourth date, where we cement the relationship, gives both the accountant and the client an opportunity to see more of each other in action before making a long-term commitment.

This isn't just a 'getting to know you' session but a full-on activity date, undertaking a project like setting up Xero, amending tax returns, catching up on tax, recommending new business structures and so on. We see each other in action, and we get to understand how each other work.

But ahead of that, let's make sure that you're making a proposal to 'the one'. Here's what we believe is the best way to articulate it:

We invite less than 50% of the businesses we meet to become a client — or join what we call the Inspire Family. To receive an invitation we need to know 3 things:

1. Is there a potential to add massive value to your business?

2. Do we share common values?

3. How will you use your business as a Force for Good.

Here's the point: having a really strong selection criteria ensures you only work with A+ Clients. [You'll see some more on that in the next chapter too.]

The proposal.

You don't quite go down on one knee, but it is here where you *'put a ring on it'* and make a proposal to have the prospect become a client. If you've done everything right through the courtship period, the relationship has blossomed, and they can't wait to say yes. It's a magical moment.

The engagement becomes official when both parties sign the terms of engagement.

The engagement.

This should be an exciting stage in the relationship, for both you and the client, and it's easy to make it so. Because at that point, you make a promise to be the perfect partner — we vow to be a proactive tax and accounting partner whose services will pay for themselves, and we let our new client know that in the past, our return on investment has averaged about four times our cost.

The engagement sets up the rest of the relationship, and your business fiancée is happy to go ahead because it won't cost them anything — in fact it will help them keep more of their hard-earned dollars.

To help you 'frame' that, let me give you the way I would describe this stage in the relationship. For us it was doing Tax and Accounting in a really special way. I positioned it as -

> Proactive Tax & Accounting that pays for itself in tax savings (4x ROI on average) and a life-changing accountant that you meet 4x a year. From $600 a month.

You get the idea. Easy to say. Easy to relate to. And, of course, easy to say 'yes!!' to. THAT's precisely the framing you need for your engagement piece too.

So, with that firmly in mind, let's get to the church for ....

The marriage.

The secret to a great and long-lasting relationship is that you keep on surprising your partner. You never get complacent, and it all starts on the wedding day — maybe six months into the engagement — when you make a new offer. This is when we invite our new client to take up our Business Co-pilot and invite them on a journey that gets them to a destination where they're working four days a week, 40 weeks a year, and extracting $400,000 or more profit per year.

At this point, the marriage is solid as a rock and both parties know it will go the distance.

To help you move to that next level, here's the wording we used back when I was at Inspire:

> Business Co-Pilot to help steer you towards working 4 days a week, 40 weeks a year, and extract $400K profit per year. From $600 a month.

And a 'yes' to that leads us to this:

Our first anniversary.

On our first anniversary (or sooner if we're both feeling the love), we then seal the deal with our offer to help the client build $4 million in prosperity across four pools of wealth that will last four generations.

Again, to help you frame your own version of this step, here's how it looked and sounded:

> Personal Co-Pilot to help steer you towards Building $4M in Wealth in 4 Pools of Wealth to last 4 Generations. From $600 a month.

As you can see, there really is power in the process.

It's a beautiful thing.

The dating/proposal/engagement/marriage/anniversary system works because it's predicated on the same things that make every successful relationship sing: hard work, respect, shared ideals and ideas, and common goals. Relationships wither and die if they aren't nurtured, so keep your eyes on the prize — happy partner, happy ever after.

THE 7-11-4 FORMULA FOR PRE-SOLD PROSPECTS

Tying the Knot isn't just a nice analogy but there's also a science to it! Whether we're shopping for corn flakes, concert tickets or a honeymoon in Paris, the Internet has changed how we decide what to buy.

Google calls this online decision-making moment 'The Zero Moment of Truth', or simply, ZMOT. The ZMOT refers to the moment in the buying process when the consumer researches a product prior to purchase.

It's now commonly understood that it takes a prospective client or buyer 7 Hours across 11 Touch Points over 4 Different Environments in order for someone to be PRE-SOLD or ready to say "YES!" to come on board as a client.

Once you 'get' this …. as in REALLY get it, you'll realise where so many firms have a lot of work to do!

In our case, for example, pre-ZMOT (and 7-11-4) we were like any typical accounting firm - we weren't published authors, we didn't run workshops / events, we weren't keynote speakers and we had no diagnostic tools like a 2nd Opinion on Tax or the Cashed Up Scorecard.

As a result we were spending 7 hours — over 11 touch points — across 4 different occasions (phone, email, in person and Zoom) one-on-one with prospects in what was a very time consuming process.

So to streamline things, to be able to do things super-efficiently and effectively, we produced some great assets (like the book, a podcast, a scorecard, Keynote presentations and workshops) to be able to 'prime' our prospects, making it so much easier for them to say YES when they're finally asked.

So a good question in your mind right now might be this: "how does 7-11-4 stack up against the 'going on a date' analogy?"

Let's take a look:

Someone hears me at Keynote at an event — 1 Hour, 1st Touch Point and 1 Environment.

They then read the Book (a gift from the above event) — 3 Hours, 2nd Touch Point and 2nd Environment.

They attend a Workshop (talking about ideas in the book) — 2 Hours, 3rd Touch Point and 3rd Environment.

They do a 2nd Opinion on Tax — 2 Hours (that's already 8 in total), 4th Touch Point and 4th Environment.

They might listen to a few episodes of the Podcast, read some of our blogs or watch some of our many videos on Facebook to clock up their remaining touch points and ...

Magically, they're ready to come on board, if we choose them!

Just like your prospects will be when you do the work (and yes, it is so much easier for Members of Life Changing Accountants to do it too.)

The question is, how well do you paint a compelling 3 to 5 year journey that you take your clients on that you can elegantly map out on one page?

Here's a simple example designed specifically for the kind of clients Inspire wanted to create. Again, this helps you build your own that really, really works too.

The Big Picture | Getting Cashed Up with Inspire

Look Under The Hood	Solve an Urgent Need				Get Cashed Up	My Family Prosperity
Second opinion on tax	Initial "Quick Win" Project	Proactive Tax & Accounting	Time saving Bookkeeping	Business coaching & advice	Wealth coaching & advice
2 Hours	First Month	Year 1 and beyond	Year 1	Year 2	Year 3
$500	POA	From $500 / m	From $300 / m	From $600 / m	From $600 / m
$500 tax savings or its free	Get the ATO off your back	$18k av annual Tax Saving	Free up 20 hours	Double Profit & Days Off	Live the Goodlife

PULL MORE MONEY TIME AND HAPPINESS FROM YOUR BUSINESS

1YR -> 3YRS

IF YOU'RE LOOKING FOR WAYS TO SAVE TAX, BOOST PROFITS & ACCELERATE CASHFLOW, YOU NEED TO LISTEN TO BEN & HARVEE

THE DRVING FORCE BEHIND INSPIRE IS TO ENSURE ALL OF THEIR CLIENTS SUCCEED IN BUSINESS AND FAMILY LIFE.

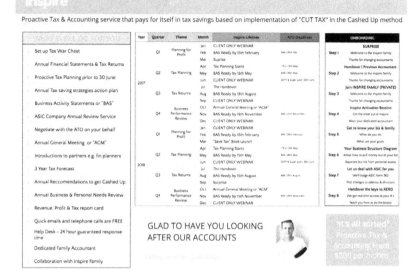

Proactive Tax & Accounting service that pays for itself in tax savings based on implementation of "CUT TAX" in the Cashed Up method

Wow, that was a journey.

So, we started with eleven touchpoints delivered over 7 hours across four environments, and we finished with a happily ever after. It's actually achievable because every step can be created by you, and where your plans differ from our tried-and-true strategies and methodologies, you can adapt.

I guess the takeaway from this chapter is that without the depth and breadth of engaging activities, opportunities and momentum that our array of touchpoints offers (see Chapter 3 U is for Unleash your IP for inspiration), you may struggle.

I would strongly urge you to consider becoming a presenter and author, because the first offers you a truly efficient gateway to prompting your prospect's *Zero Moment of Truth*, and the latter provides an effective way of creating and delivering so many of the touchpoints you need to get them into the 'yes' zone.

Or, you could go back to buying people coffee and gathering new clients one croissant and a thousand calories at a time.

WANNA GO ON A DATE?

Thinking of Changing Accountants? Let's just take it easy and go on a few dates first to see if each other is 'the one'.

FIRST DATE

Learn about the 7 Smart Financial Decisions of a Cashed Up Business by Ben Walker & Harvee Pene with the **Cashed Up Book, Workshop & Scorecard.**

SECOND DATE

Let's take the next step by doing a **"Look Under the Hood"**. A $500 2nd Opinion on Tax, guaranteed to find $500 in tax savings or it's free.

THIRD DATE

Let's complete an "Urgent Need" project upfront to help claw back $$$'s in overpaid tax, get up to date with the ATO and / or set up NEW business structures.

THE PROPOSAL

We invite less than 50% of the Businesses we meet to become a client - or what we call 'join the Inspire Family'. To receive an invitation we need to know -

1 - Is there potential to ADD MASSIVE VALUE TO YOUR BUSINESS?
2 - Do we SHARE COMMON VALUES?
3 - How will you use your BUSINESS FOR GOOD?

IT'S ALL SORTED

Proactive Tax & Accounting that pays for itself in Tax Savings (av. 4 x ROI) & a Life Changing Accountant that you see 4 x times a year, to help you make Smart Financial Decisions. Starts at $600 / month + GST.

TOTAL FINANCIAL CONTROL

Proactive Financial Co-Pilot (Business) to help you Work 4 Days a Week, 40 Weeks a Year & Pull $400K+ Profit per Year. Starts at $600 / month + GST.

THE GOOD LIFE

Proactive Financial Co-Pilot (Personal) to help you Build $4M+ in 4 Pools of Wealth to Last 4 Generations. Starts at $600 / month + GST.

inspire.business   1300 852 747   hello@inspireca.com

108

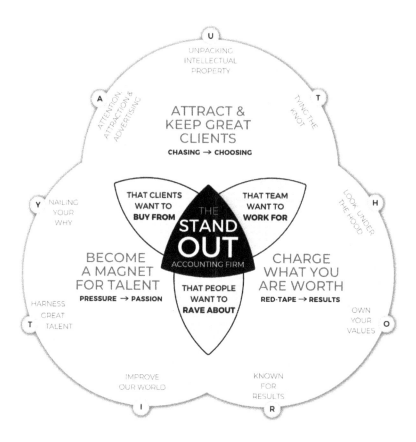

CHAPTER 5
H is for Look under the Hood

Welcome to the chapter that gives you the opportunity to shine. So far, we've talked about things you can do to build your brand, spread awareness of your offering, and multiply the effect by packaging your IP and making it available to a wider audience without you having to lift a finger.

In this chapter, you get to show your chops, so to speak. Formulate your own strategy and put in the hard yards to bring the prospect one step closer to becoming a client. The *Look Under the Hood* is all about how you interact with the people you want to become your clients, and what you deliver that makes them want to do more business with you.

Consider that everything that's gone before has been the art of getting people to discover your restaurant, peruse the menu and decide to make a booking. All those videos, blogs and vlogs, every touchpoint that they've encountered so far, amount to the appetisers — the free cheese sticks and olives you put on the table. Nice little nibbles that sharpen the appetite but aren't filling and don't showcase your ability to produce something both tempting and tasty.

The *Look Under the Hood* is the entrée that proves to them that you really know your way around the kitchen. Its up to you to create something so more-ish, so irresistible, that they come back for more.

Action Plan

Look Under The Hood	Solve an Urgent Need				Get Cashed Up	My Family Prosperity
Second opinion on tax	Initial "Quick Win" Project	Proactive Tax & Accounting	Time saving Bookkeeping	Business coaching & advice	Wealth coaching & advice
2 Hours	First Month	Year 1 and beyond	Year 1	Year 2	Year 3
$500	POA	From $500 / m	From $300 / m	From $600 / m	From $600 / m
$500 tax savings or its free	Get the ATO off your back	$18k av. annual Tax Saving	Free up 20 hours	Double Profit & Days Off	Live the Goodlife

You're working towards posing a challenging question to the prospect you're courting here: you're going to ask them to fire their old accountant and appoint you to take proactive charge of their business and financial affairs.

It's human nature that they'll resist. Even if they suspect that they aren't getting the value they should out of their current accountant, even if they complain about them at every opportunity, most people will be reluctant to make the break. It requires a confronting moment with someone they've dealt with and quite likely trusted for years, followed immediately by a leap into the unknown. Just picture yourself changing banks, phone companies or internet service providers and you'll know exactly what I mean. It's enough to freak anybody out.

So the last thing you want to do is come straight out and ask your potential new client to drop the old bean counter and appoint you. You have to coax them into coming up with the idea of appointing you themselves, and the *Look Under the Hood* is the means to that end.

Once you get your potential new customer to agree to giving you a look under their hood, so to speak, you've brought them onto your turf. Your expertise and experience will come to the fore, and you'll have one chance to get it right.

The first thing to look at.

The *Look Under the Hood* isn't just an opportunity to find tax savings for the prospective new client — it's an opportunity for you to look under *their* hood and see if they're the kind of person or business you really want to deal with. You have a unique ability to see into their financial management, and that gives you an insight into what sort of people are behind it, and whether they share your values. This is crucial, because it's a way of vetting the customer before they become a customer — you get to suss them out while they're sussing you out. And if you like what you see, then you have an opportunity to groom them as a new client.

Another crucial point.

The key to turning a *Look Under the Hood* into a new customer — if you deem them worthy! — is in what you deliver. It must be so good that they'll undertake the distasteful duty of firing their old accountant, and then hand over years of private information to you, someone they barely know. And that part is up to you. I can give you a structure to follow. I can give you advice on how to persuade people to give you that shot, and help you make sure the environment you greet them in is designed to inspire confidence and tribal solidarity with you. But you'll have to do the grunt work that brings them home. I hope you're ready.

So just what is this magical pathway?

Every day in accounting firm offices all over the world, qualified and highly experienced accountants give away their intellectual property in the form of free advice — often in the hope of winning a client. Hands up if you've ever spent hours with a tyre-kicker who walked away from a meeting with you armed with a load of great ideas, and no intention of ever seeing you again.

It's partly due to the fact that you've under-estimated the value of such a conversation, and partly because you're an accountant (not a salesperson) that you let this happen.

The *Look Under the Hood* is about changing that. It gives you a simple structure to work with, and an easily understood and quickly proven proposition for the customer — backed with a guarantee.

The pointy end.

In a nutshell, you make the prospective client an offer they can't refuse — for just $500 you'll conduct a *Look Under the Hood* of some description, and you *guarantee* that what you uncover in savings will more than cover the cost of the exercise.

Get $100 of a 2nd Opinion on your Tax
Guaranteed to find $500 in tax savings, *or it's free.*

Got a feeling you're paying too much tax?

Don't miss out on a 2nd Opinion on your Tax from "Australia's most impactful Accounting firm". Here's how it works -

1. Get a $500 2nd Opinion on Tax, less $100 bonus.
2. Send us your most recent Tax Returns & Financial Statements.
3. We review your Tax, within 48 hours.
4. If we can't find $500+ Tax Savings? We'll give your $$ back.
5. We usually find $600 - $60K in Tax Savings ... Happy Days

If you think you're paying too much tax or that it's time to change accountants. Start with a 2nd Opinion.

You don't think the Tax Man deserves a tip do you?

We use the Tax Savings concept — we'll find $500 or more in tax savings, or you pay nothing. That's a huge earner for us, because we almost never fail, and in fact usually determine that the client could have saved many thousands of dollars if they'd been with us in the first place.

Tax savings aren't the only mechanism you can use here — a good friend of ours promises that for $500 he will find at least $1000 in cash flow savings or the customer pays nothing. But for now, we'll stick with the tax savings approach we use, because we know it so well.

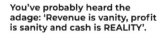

You've probably heard the adage: 'Revenue is vanity, profit is sanity and cash is REALITY'.

And it's true.

It turns out there are only 7 Key Levers you can pull to unlock more Cash, Profit and Revenue (interestingly, we call that 'CPR') from your business.

P is for Pricing

R is for Revenues

O is for Overheads

F is for Cashflow

I is for a Return on Your Investment

T is for the Time you spend working

S is for Surplus

An investment in a 'CPR Review' is just $500 and it comes with a promise to find at least 10 times that by making a few small changes according to our P.R.O.F.I.T.S. Methodology

It starts with a question.

Getting people I'd like to work with to agree to a *Look Under the Hood* is easy, because I use a well-known and terribly aggravating pain point as my entry.

"Do you ever get the feeling that you're paying too much tax?"

YOU DON'T REALLY THINK THE TAX MAN DESERVES A TIP DO YOU?

I know, right?! Who in their right minds can honestly ever answer "no" (except for my clients, of course)? It's an idea that worms its way into your brain and niggles at you day and night, and it won't go away. Because the very idea that you're paying too much tax is like a genuine pain. It's awful.

If your prospect is a trusting individual like me, when they're asked that question and even when they can't avoid answering in the affirmative, their mind will throw up all sorts of roadblocks to the next logical step — the understanding that, perhaps through complacency, failure to keep up with the changes in their business and their life, because they're busy or whatever, their accountant hasn't been as attentive or as competent as they should be to the person's tax management. Your prospect might even say to themselves that getting a second opinion on their tax would in some way be cheating on their accountant. Who, after all has been with them for years and is a wonderful person and they wouldn't want to offend them and...well you know the rest.

But when the question is put with an offer — a Second Opinion on your tax with a guarantee of finding $500 or more in savings, the allure is just too great for most people. And for those whose loyalty to their accountant (or their fear of firing them) is so great that they'd rather go on paying too much tax — well, good luck to them, I say.

This may help to avoid the hurt.

Incidentally, very often when you put the offer to a prospective client and they agree to a *Look Under the Hood*, there will be one more barrier — the information you need to complete the *Look* (tax records, financials) will almost always reside with the old accountant. So rather than strain their relationship with their accountant by admitting they're getting a second opinion, I tell my *Look Under the Hood* clients to always, be respectful of your current relationship with your accountant when asking for access to the required information.

That way, on those extremely rare occasions when our relationship with them doesn't work out, there's no ill feeling between them and their existing accountant.

Making it happen.

The *Look Under the Hood* is your first chance to provide a concrete service for your prospective client and prove to them what you can do. It's probably the most critical touchpoint of them all — after the *Zero Moment of Truth* that gets them interested in you. It's therefore absolutely crucial that you employ every means possible to get them to sign up for the *Look*.

This is, again, where all your hard work in making signature presentations and hosting events, partnerships, referrals, social media and so on pay off. Every time you appear on a stage or screen, you have a ready-made audience, many of whom have already been exposed to your message of being impact-driven and are receptive to the idea of you proving that you can walk the walk as well as you talk the talk.

But that doesn't mean you can just ask and you will receive. This isn't an "if you build it, they will come" moment. You have to provide all the encouragement, incentives and inducements you can.

Collateral rocks.

That's why I carry a suitcase full of customisable and licensable *Look Under the Hood* collateral everywhere I go — because I never know when I will meet that golden prospect and want to bring them on board.

So as the old American Express ad used to say, don't leave home without it — in my case a bundle of brochures, merchandise, sales scripts, checklists, and a fair bit of other stuff, and the most important tool of all, Gift Cards.

Gift Cards rule.

Whenever the opportunity to do so presents itself — and I find a lot of such opportunities — I hand out Gift Cards entitling the bearer to $100 Off the cost of a signature Second Opinion on Tax under our *Look Under the Hood* branding.

They cost me about 70 cents each (I have a LOT of these things printed and they are genuine gift cards like the ones you might see at the department stores or supermarkets), and I give a LOT of them away, but every time I do I say to myself that I'm happy to give away 70 cents to get a $400 job, and possibly a lifelong customer.

The gift of giving.

Imagine you've just spoken at an event, and everyone is busy giving out business cards — and then you start handing out $100 Gift Cards. The effect is amazing. I often play a game where I offer someone a Gift Card. I say, "do you know someone who would benefit from getting $100 off a Look Under the Hood signature Second Opinion on their tax?" and hold out one card. Almost every time, they ask for more than one, and I'm happy to give them a handful, because it boosts the chances of them giving us a referral.

Of course, one of the most fruitful and exciting times to offer Gift Cards like these is at times when the person I'm speaking to is on an emotional high. Like when I've just sent them their Magic Number message or been through their tax savings in a *Look Under the Hood* delivery meeting. At times like that, I can't give them away fast enough.

The Magic Number.

I've mentioned the Magic Number before, and it's pretty easy to guess what it's about. When we've done our due diligence and been through the potential client's tax returns to see where they could have saved tax, we come up with a number, usually between $600 and $60,000 in savings. That's the Magic Number.

Now, as with everything else we do, there's a science to

revealing this Magic Number. If we wait until the delivery meeting, we can get unexpected emotions bubbling to the surface. These can range from disbelief to questioning our integrity ("surely to get a number that high you'd have to do something dodgy?"), to anger at their old accountant that clouds their decision-making, to blinding euphoria.

So a couple of days before the delivery meeting, we send them a message saying, in effect, *we've found your Magic Number and it's $xx,xxx*. The reason we do it this way is that it heightens their sense of anticipation for the delivery meeting — suddenly they're super keen to attend — and because it gives them a couple of days to work through those emotions and formulate the questions they'll need to ask ("surely to get a number that high you'd have to do something dodgy?" Not in the least, and I can explain why…).

The delivery meeting.

The delivery meeting is a massive event for the prospect and for us. It's the first time they see us in action talking specifically about their own situation and giving, in precise detail, the actions we can take on their behalf to save them from paying too much tax. So we want to make everything about the meeting perfect.

The meeting environment.

Walk into an accountant's offices almost anywhere in the world and you'll see pretty much the same things — maybe a couple of qualifications on the wall, perhaps a print of a landscape. Kinda uninspiring, right?

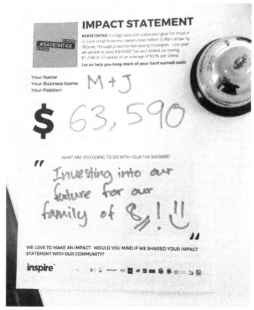

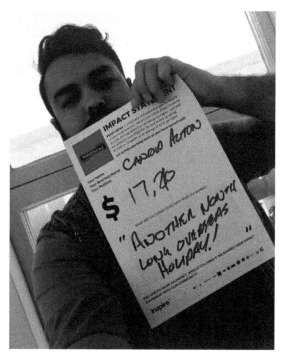

When people walked into our offices, they saw evidence of our impact plastered all over the walls. Pictures of our celebrations when we reached a tax saving goal (once upon a time it was $1 million, but then it got up over $10 million), and milestones for our giving (for every tax dollar we saved we gave a day of access to clean water to people who needed it, so we'd given away a lot of days!).

It's impossible for our visitors not to have seen these things, and we got a lot of comments about them — after all, we're doing exactly what we said we would way back when we committed to being a business for good.

In the meeting room, there's more of the same, but we left plenty of Gift Cards on the table as well, and we made sure our visitors knew they could help themselves.

The delivery.

Our *Look Under the Hood* second opinion on tax demands that we do some serious digging into the prospective client's tax affairs. We cover ten areas of their finances and structure that we know from experience will yield good or more frequently great results.

Importantly, our investigations are *not* exhaustive. This is partly because that would take far more time than we are prepared to invest in a $500 (or $400 with Gift Card) return, and partly because it leaves us room to find more savings once we are appointed as their accountants.

We rate our prospect's previous return/s on a range of issues from claiming accelerated depreciation to paying tax on money not yet received and the benefits of pre-paying certain commitments, and we consider their business structure and ways that they might save tax by updating it.

The report.

On the day, a few days after we've already revealed the Magic Number, we provide the prospect with a printed report, which is naturally carefully constructed. If our meeting is online, we express post their printed report to them — it's vital that they have something tangible in their hands.

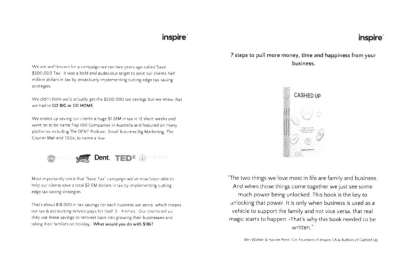

In the first page or two, we introduce ourselves and talk about our philosophy and our commitment to impact and being a business for good. It's important to reinforce that message every chance we get, because it's so effective at recruiting like-minded people.

The Magic Number (again).

Then we devote a whole page to the Magic Number, and we ask them for an impact statement: What are you going to do with that extra money? This really gets them engaged and makes the Magic Number real money that they can spend or use for whatever purpose they have in mind. Often it gets them thinking — surrounded as they are by our tales of impact — on how they may be able to use some of that money for good.

In the subsequent pages we explain how we arrived at their Magic Number figure. We talk about their business structure and how changing that could reduce their tax vulnerability, and we canvass other ways in which they might save money.

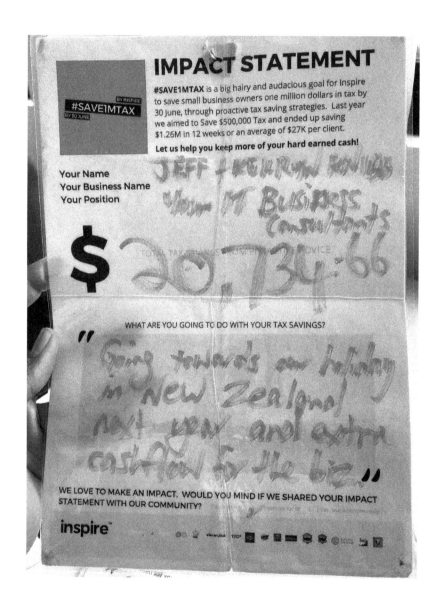

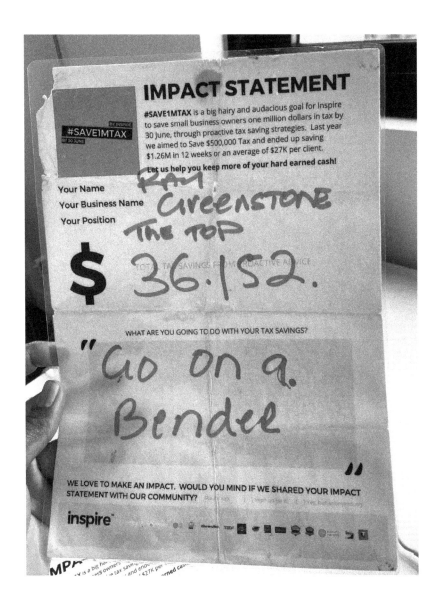

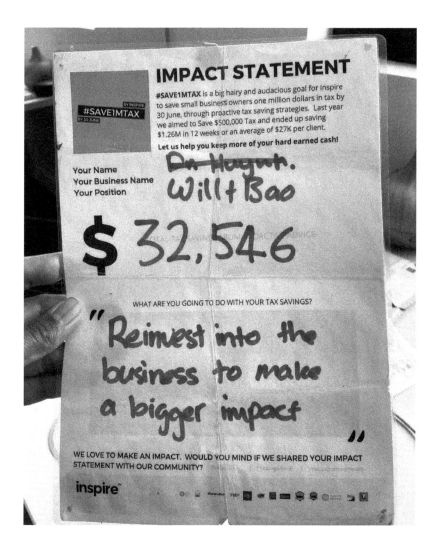

The "true cost" shock.

Next, we sum up the "true cost" of their current accountant by adding that accountant's fees to the extra tax paid, to show a truly alarming figure. A figure like that can come as quite a shock.

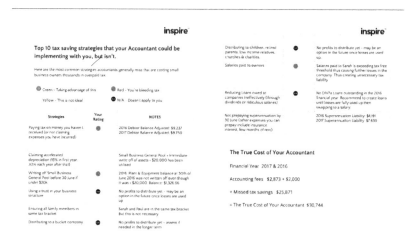

In the discussion that follows, we talk about our fees in the context of the value we deliver, and in contrast to the true cost of their current situation. You can almost feel them warming to us and becoming more and more disenchanted with their unpalatable status quo.

The action plan.

Still, even though they are now well and truly in our territory and often physically leaning in — a classic body language "tell" — we don't just come right out and ask for their business. Instead, we introduce an action plan, which is designed to "solve an urgent need" or two. This includes amending their previous tax returns to get the refunds they deserve and preparing the current year's tax return to ensure that they get all of the tax savings we've located.

At this point we also invite them to subscribe to one of our services, which we explain is based on the value we provide rather than the hours we spend on it and give examples of the kind of return on investment they can expect.

inspire™

Action Plan

Look Under The Hood	Solve an Urgent Need			Get Cashed Up	My Family Prosperity
Second opinion on tax	Initial "Quick Win" Project	Proactive Tax & Accounting	Time saving Bookkeeping	Business coaching & advice	Wealth coaching & advice
2 Hours	First Month	Year 1 and beyond	Year 1	Year 2	Year 3
$500	POA	From $500 / m	From $300 / m	From $600 / m	From $600 / m
$500 tax savings or its free	Get the ATO off your back	$18k av. annual Tax Saving	Free up 20 hours	Double Profit & Days Off	Live the Good life

PULL MORE MONEY TIME AND HAPPINESS FROM YOUR BUSINESS

1YR --➤ 3YRS

Priorities	Cost	Timing	Value
**Solve an Urgent Need	Initial "Quick Win" Project** Amend 2016 financial year tax returns and financial statements Amend Sarah's Individual Tax Return Amend June 2016 BAS Amend Payment Summary Statement	$1,000 + GST	2 weeks	Immediate benefit: $9,209 in cash refund
**Solve an Urgent Need	Prepare 2017 Tax Return** - ████Pty Ltd - Sarah████(Amend)	$2,250 +GST	2 weeks	Prepare 2017 tax returns within 2 weeks and save estimated $16,662
Subscribe to 'It's All Sorted' *A proactive tax & accounting service that pays for itself in tax savings. For:* ████Pty Ltd -Sarah██	$2,250 + GST upfront & $500 + GST / mth	1st of April	

It's a done deal.

By the time we've completed the urgent tasks on the action plan and obtained the refunds and savings that the client has a right to, they are generally well and truly convinced. The deal is done.

I can't stress enough the importance of the *Look Under the Hood* in gaining new business, and you can see from the detail included here that it's an exacting process that requires proper design and construction.

The good news is, once you've created, trialled and evolved your *Look Under the Hood* and its associated offer, you can train your staff to deliver the elements involved, and you can spend your days dealing with the needs of your growing client list.

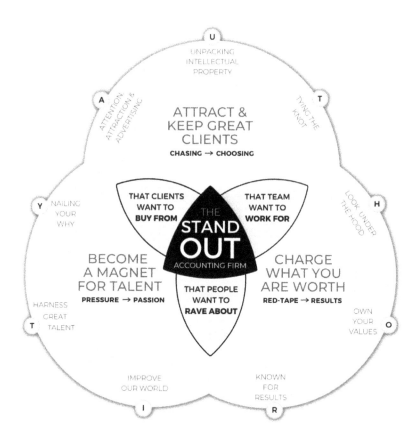

CHAPTER 6
O is for Own your Values

We've already spoken a lot about values in this book, and in this chapter they come to the fore once again. Because I know what it's like to put value over values, and to regret the necessity of that choice. Saying yes to jobs you don't want to do or to working with people you really don't want to work with because you need the turnover is a difficult and humiliating position to be in. But we've all been there, and at least that phase in our lives provides a hard-won but much-appreciated lesson.

So I want you to make a commitment, right here and now, to own your values. By that I mean speak them proudly, share them with anyone who will listen and most of all live by them. Take a vow never to sacrifice your values for money again. I can guarantee you that it will be like lifting a weight off your shoulders, and it will make the rest of your business and personal life so much simpler and more enjoyable.

Learn to say no.

What I am talking about here is putting yourself in the position of authority. Giving yourself permission to live up to the ideals you profess and choosing only to deal with people and businesses that share your values. And learning that it's okay to say no. When you give yourself the authority to say no, you gain the respect and deference of people who will happily walk all over you if you say nothing but yes.

In my experience, people who say no more often hear yes much more often, because everyone knows where you stand, and where they stand. There is certainly a mutual respect that often leads to shared ideals and values.

Say goodbye to troublesome clients.

The main purpose of taking a 'values first' stand, apart from the boost it gives your self-esteem and the drive that it lends to your business, is that it gives you the authority to choose who you work with, and to simply say no to troublesome clients.

We all know who they are: they're slow to respond but they always need things urgently. They don't provide the information we need within the timeframes required, if at all, and then they have the audacity to complain when things are lodged later than anticipated.

On the other hand, leading with your values allows you to be up front with your clients about *their* values, and to set some ground rules around your relationship. The people who share your values and who will treat you with the consideration you deserve will readily agree to your terms, because they recognise that the relationship is based on a meeting of the minds and a platform of common ethics. The people who don't agree to your terms are the ones you want to run away from — fast.

Say hello to like-minded people.

When you wear your values on your sleeve, so to speak, you attract people who think and act the same way you do. They respond to you with positivity and high regard and they become genuine partners in business rather than being out for whatever they can get from you.

When you take the next step and become a business for good, people will be drawn to your good works, but also to your commitment and your outlook. Committing to creating an impact and becoming a business for good inevitably makes you think positively and act that way too. I can't tell you how powerful it is for us to give away access to clean water every time we save a client a dollar in tax — it's a huge motivation for us, and it makes us smile.

So when you decide you want to deal with people like us (like you!), own your values. Take a stand to stand out — and let the world know how you feel. These days, when we start to assess that a business owner really does have the potential to be 'one of us', and we invite them to be a client, we ask them to sign an agreement with us. We sign it in their presence too, because it's a mutual commitment we're making. It starts us off on the right foot by setting out the terms of our relationship and ensures that we're on the same page as far as values and actions go.

Dream big. Make an impact. Remember your roots.

That's the subheading to the *8 Agreements of the Inspire Family*, and it set the tone for the whole document. Here's the agreement in full, with a few notes on each clause:

*We promise to be **proactive**,*
*if you promise to be **reactive**.*

We promise to proactively reach out to you every month with an idea or strategy on how you can Save Tax, Boost Profits and/or Accelerate Cashflow. That's our responsibility to you as your Trusted Advisor. This proactivity is why we've been able to save our clients on average $18,000+ in tax savings — or 3 x their investment in our Tax & Accounting Service. But to pull off this magic, we need you to work with us.

- *Please respond to us when we need you to (24 — 48 hours would be great).*
- *Please give us access to the information we need (we can't start a job until we have everything).*
- *Please take personal responsibility if we miss a deadline with the Australian Tax Office (ATO)because you couldn't get things to us in time.*

We like to maintain our 100% early lodgement service with the ATO and if slow responses or lack of information holds us up, we both get in their bad books.

Early lodgement means you know well in advance how to cashflow what is owed to the ATO or get your refund earlier.

See how we set out the first of those terms in a friendly, accessible tone? We're not asking for the world here, just for the client to treat us with the same consideration we promise to them.

Stop doing the books, and start doing better business

We *reckon there are better things you could be doing with your time than doing your bookkeeping. The average business owner spends 10 — 20 hours per month doing bookkeeping, which we believe could be better reinvested back into your business and your life. So maybe not year one, but definitely from year two onwards we want you to give up the bookkeeping and either engage Inspire to do it or another quality bookkeeper — either way your DIY bookkeeping days are numbered...*

This came from an internal goal that no client would ever do their own bookkeeping. In pursuit of saving a few dollars, most of them did the bookkeeping wrong, which meant more time and less efficiency for us. And for the few who actually were good at bookkeeping, the opportunity cost was still too high.

One of our favourite clients — a dentist — did his own bookkeeping and was amazing at it. But seriously, was it worth the 2 hours a week for him when he could have been spending time with family or working *in* or *on* his business? That's why we introduced the *'your bookkeeping days are numbered'* policy — we promised to do just as good a job as our dentist friend, or better, and to free up his time. It worked.

Become a Business for Good

We believe that business should be the driving force behind creating a better world. That's why as we help you get Cashed Up — by making smarter financial decisions — we will encourage you to find ways to give back and become what we call a 'Business for Good' — one that gives part of its profits to making the world a better place. We've partnered with global giving initiative B1G1 Business for Good to make business giving easy. We highly recommend you do that too.

We've always known that the client / accountant relationship is very intimate (financially), so it only makes sense that we share the same goals and values.

So we decided that we would own our values to the extent that we would ask every client we worked with to embrace Business as a Force for Good, The UN Global Goals, B1G1.com, The 1% Pledge or some form of 'Purpose Beyond Profit'. We could be sure that the clients who were happy to sign were our kind of people — and those that wouldn't, probably weren't and we agreed to part ways. That's the strength of our commitment, and the power of saying no.

Talk about us behind our back!

Some of our best clients have come from referrals — a.k.a. when we do a good job and clients talk about us behind our backs. For the first time in our lives, this is actually a good thing. We would hope that after we've delivered some great value to you (Save Tax, Boost Profits, Accelerate Cashflow) that you will give consideration to referring us to at least 2 other business people who you believe would benefit from the work we do.

Historically, referrals have been the most popular way for accounting firms to grow their business. The trouble is most accounting firms that I saw never had a program on how to do it — how to systematically request referrals from happy clients. So we set up the relationship from day one with the expectation of at least 2 referrals … and because of this, we ended up getting close to 5 each year from each client.

We love you, but we won't go to jail for you

If you want us to do anything illegal, shady or unethical, we're definitely NOT the right accountant for you. That involves not declaring cash, claiming deductions that aren't allowed or crossing the line of the law. We'll help you execute every legally available strategy to help you save tax, but we're not in the game of doing anything illegal. You cool with that?

Yes, we've all had those clients who expect us to do something 'dodgy', shady or downright illegal. We won't be put in that position. That's why we embedded this 'we love you, but we won't go to jail for you' clause in our agreement. Ironically, because of the values-led marketing we had done, none of our clients ever expected us to go too close to the line. But after reading this agreement, those who had high levels of integrity felt even safer going ahead with us.

> ### Please pay your bills on time
>
> *If we're delivering what we promised and you aren't paying your bills on time, then the laws of exchange are out of balance. And that's not fair on everyone else who is paying on time, or our Team, who are working hard for you.*
>
> *So if your account is more than 7 days in arrears, we'll attempt to charge your card without further notice. If payments continue to be unsuccessful, we'll have to limit your access to our service until you are up to date.*

We've never really had any issues with clients paying us on time, but maybe that's because we said this upfront (in fact, lots of clients asked if they could use this phrasing in their businesses!).

Be a good human.

There is no room for rude, insulting or general bad behaviour and anyone being anything other than a cool human will be asked to leave the Inspire Family. This goes for clients (you) as well as our Inspire Team and Business Partners.

As with late payments, we've never really had any issues with rude clients, but the fact that we were so upfront about the importance of being a good human made the 'good humans' reading this feel more at ease and at more comfortable in doing business with us.

You get what you pay for.

When you join the "It's all sorted" tax and accounting service, you get:

- *Set up Tax War Chest*
- *Annual Financial Statements & Tax Returns*
- *Proactive Tax Planning prior to 30 June*
- *Annual Tax saving strategies action plan*
- *Business Activity Statements or "BAS"*
- *ASIC Company Annual Review Service*
- *Negotiate with the ATO on your behalf*
- *Annual General Meeting or "AGM"*
- *Introductions to partners e.g. fin planners*
- *3 Year Tax Forecast*

- *Annual Recommendations to get Cashed Up*
- *Annual Business & Personal Needs Review*
- *Quick emails and telephone calls are FREE*
- *Help Desk — 24 hour guaranteed response time*
- *Dedicated Family Account*
- *Collaboration with Inspire Family*

We'll more than happily have a quick phone call or answer an email (within 24 hours or so) but if something falls out of scope, we'll do the right thing and give you an upfront price for that project.

The partners like financial planners or mortgage brokers that we may introduce you to also work on the same understanding of everything agreed up front.

Some examples of projects or advice that fall outside the scope of tax and accounting (unless it has been separately included in your proposal) —

- *Bookkeeping*
- *Payroll*
- *Xero Training*
- *Advice on CGT of an asset — selling a property or business*
- *Setting up a new structure*
- *Structure Advice*
- *Preparing business performance reports such as P & L,*
- *Balance Sheet or a Business Budget.*

- *Preparing financial reports for your board meeting or award application.*
- *QBCC Review or Audit Submission*
- *Business Software Review*

We introduced this clause because "scope creep" can be a massive productivity and profit killer, so we needed to be upfront about what exactly was included and clear examples of what was not included. The product brochure/ engagement letter already covered these inclusions, but it's always a good idea to reconfirm in writing what the client is getting when they sign up.

My promise to you

I promise to return your phone call or email within 24 hours — outside of weekends and public holidays or unforeseen circumstances.

I promise to treat you like I would my family. That means that I won't recommend anything to you that I wouldn't recommend to my mother or sister. It also means that if I don't think what you're doing is a good idea I'll let you know.

I promise to be your trusted advisor. This means I'll keep everything we say and everything I know about your family and your business in confidence. It also means I'll do everything in my power to help you make smarter financial decisions.

The sign off is the most important vow of all — the promise to be a trusted and confidential advisor. We, the client and the accountant, read this paragraph together, and the promise is made sincerely while looking the client straight in the eye.

Before we move on.

There's a lot of detail around what we're recommending here that we've had to gloss over a bit because of restrictions on space and your reading time. But that doesn't make it any less important. Owning your values, committing to making an impact and becoming a business for good are some of the most important and influential steps you'll take in your business life, so I am hoping you'll be inspired to read further on them. I also hope you'll take the time to examine, understand, codify and present your values to the world, because that's the first step in gaining the power of owning your values.

As far as being a business for good goes, there's more on that in the next couple of chapters and I hope you'll be motivated by what you find in them.

CHAPTER 7

R is for Raising your Reputation through R.E.S.U.L.T.S.

In the last chapter, we spoke about owning your values and how it will change your approach to your business. In this chapter, we'll be showing you how the results you achieve can make a massive impact on your reputation.

The basic issue here is that when you move to being driven by impact, you set goals for what you want to achieve — and when you set goals, you can monitor your progress towards those goals. And once you start measuring your impact, the results you can accumulate can be mind-blowing. You find that you genuinely can change lives — starting with your clients, but quickly expanding to changing the lives of people you'll never even meet.

But before we get a rush of blood to the head over the impact making an impact can have on your life and business, let's get to some basics first.

What does it take to stand out?

I once asked an advertising person I knew, who has somehow survived decades in that crazy business, *what is the one thing about your job that drives you nuts.* Without hesitating, he launched into a story about what the ad industry calls the USP — the Unique Sales Proposition.

The theory behind this is sound: you figure out what makes your business genuinely unique — in other words makes it different enough to stand out from its competitors — and you use that to build the campaign, or the brand personality, or whatever. The trouble, according to my friend, who had begun to twitch a little by then, is that "every client I ever met, when I asked them what made them different, said 'oh that would be our service.' Now, when every single competitor in your industry is claiming that 'service' is their USP, then it is no longer a *Unique* Sales Proposition but a *Universal* Sales Proposition. It's madness to try and stand out using the same alleged quality as everyone else in your field. It's like claiming that your milk is different because it's white!"

The lesson here is that we as accountants are prone to thinking that what sets us apart is usually one of five different aspects of our offering:

1. Price

2. Quality

3. Professionalism

4. Relationships (service)

5. Proactivity

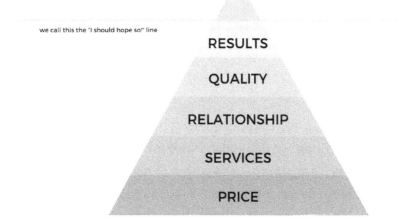

WHAT'S ABOVE THE LINE FOR YOU?

we call this the "I should hope so!" line

RESULTS

QUALITY

RELATIONSHIP

SERVICES

PRICE

These are all admirable qualities for an accounting business to possess, but they are not and will never be worthy of being used as a USP. Why not? Because, like the ubiquitous 'service' that drove my friend to distraction, these are not unique qualities that the customer is looking for, they are standard aspects of the accounting business that the customer *expects you to have in abundance*.

Now, when we are asked what our Unique Sales Proposition is, we answer "Impact" — and the tangible aspect of that, which we use to verify and promote our USP, is *Results*.

In some ways, the impact we make is unique to us because we choose the ways in which we are a business for good, so the results we get are also unique — they have our own individual stamp on them.

But…there are some aspects of our impact that can be applied to any accountancy business, and tailored to that firm's unique philosophy and drives, and we call them…

R.E.S.U.L.T.S.

Take a look at thebucketlistaccountant.com.au — this business is one we've worked with for some time, and their website is a consummate example of how to track, promote and make use of the impact they're making. Imagine the effect when potential clients see the numbers on that website. It's astounding. And you could be presenting your success in precisely the same way!

As members of Life Changing Accountants, we hereby make a public commitment to be driven by one thing:

MAKING AN IMPACT

An impact on the businesses and lives of our clients, and together with them an impact in our communities and our world.

Our commitment, not surprisingly, is a total commitment to stand by the results that we create for our clients where results stands for -

SO THAT we can proactively help our clients reach

THE RESULTS BENCHMARK

DOING 4 DAYS A WEEK
WORKING 40 WEEKS A YEAR
PULLING 400K PROFIT p.a.
BUILDING 4M WEALTH
LASTING 4 GENERATIONS

Committing to making an impact is the first step to creating your unique brand. What 'good' you choose to do, how you achieve your results and how you promote them are entirely up to you. But to get you started, let's take a look at some areas where you can make an impact, and what that will mean.

R is for Increased Revenue

$ 112,354,167

TOTAL INCREASE IN CLIENT REVENUES

Revenues

The goal here is to increase the volume of business your client gets, and the value of that increased flow of revenue. It could be as simple as giving them the peace of mind to get on with their work knowing that you have their accounting firmly and proactively in hand, or as complex as helping them develop new markets, target new clients or understand SPEARS better. Whatever your involvement, increasing your clients' revenues will increase your value to them, and you'll reap the rewards in your own revenue growth. See how quickly a change in focus to impact can change everything?

Equity

The greater the positive impact you can have on a business, the more valuable that business becomes, and the greater the value of your client's equity. When you help to grow the value of a business, your actions and the results they bring don't go unnoticed. Your commitment to the future of their business makes you more valuable to the individuals who make the decisions.

Surplus

It's one thing to increase revenue, it's another to increase surplus revenue. You can help by assisting your clients in cutting costs, saving tax, improving cash flow and more — and the more surplus you can produce, the higher your value to the client's business. It's a win/win situation.

U is for Contribution to UN Global Goals

3,120,356

TOTAL GIVING IMPACTS VIA B1G1 BUSINESS FOR GOOD

U.N.

This is a seemingly altruistic impact, but one that raises the esteem your clients have for you, creates real and achievable goals for your team members, and helps the globe we live on. It's all about committing to the United Nations Global Goals for Sustainable Development. Everyone we work with who does this finds it gives their whole organisation a lift in productivity, commitment and satisfaction — and that includes client satisfaction.

Liabilities

Limiting their liabilities — identifying slow payers who disrupt the cash flow and bring the business down, recommending pre-paying certain costs that reduce tax obligations, finding ways to cut costs — can enhance your value to your clients. When you make an impact here, your advice and assistance become indispensable.

Tax

Tax savings are the Holy Grail of our industry and the lifeblood of your clients' businesses. When you get proactive about saving your clients' tax, they notice, and they increase their reliance on your expertise because their trust in you is boosted. But don't just offer to "cut tax", make a goal — mirror what we've done and share in our success. You'll find out more below.

Scaling

You'd be surprised how few clients are acquainted with tactics like scaling their cash flow to suit their business model — they just don't have your insights in issues like these. So you can step in and educate them proactively. Teach them to pay attention to how long clients take to pay and what effect that has on their business. When you give them the benefit of your experience in related areas like borrowing and interest, and business structure and ownership, you're giving them more air to breathe.

Being paid your worth.

If you can make an impact on your clients' businesses across all these areas, suddenly you're very different from and much more valued than their previous accountant. It's not your time they should be paying for here, but the value you add to their business. If you help a client grow their business, save cashflow and reduce tax obligations to the tune of, say $50,000 a year (and that's a conservative objective), shouldn't you get paid for your contribution?

The traditional approach to accounting is to charge the client for the time it takes to meet their compliance requirements, and to give away the advice that might help them. It's a terrible model.

That's why when you move to an impact-driven model, you need to change your attitude to your own income. By packaging the advice you used to give away into income producing modules, and by measuring and reporting on the difference you're making to your clients' businesses, you're proving your value to them every single day.

So you need to be paid accordingly. The old way of adding up the cost of the hours spent and adding a small amount for administration and profit, is just unfair to you. Your new approach should be to charge, as we do, Cost + Value. As I mentioned above, if your impact on a business is to create a positive difference of $50,000 a year, why wouldn't you calculate your value at, say $10,000? The client is still miles in front, and they understand that they're paying for your intellectual property, your experience and your proactivity — not just the time you spent filling in tax forms.

In other words, to make an impact on your own business, make an impact on your clients' businesses.

Get tracking.

If you're reading this — and I know you are because you're reading *this* — I assume that you are an accomplished, experienced and ambitious accountant. So I am not going to presume to tell you how to go about achieving most of the R.E.S.U.L.T.S. laid out above.

Things like cash flow, revenue, liabilities and taxation savings are, or should be, things you know a fair bit about. The only difference this chapter can make to how you deal with those things is in how you perceive the value of your experience and your right to charge for it.

If you're like most accountants and you give away your advice for free, neither you nor your clients value it so much, because it's free. Which means neither of you are likely to pay too much attention to what effect your advice has on your client's business.

So my purpose here is not to tell you how to do those things, but to show you how to get the most mileage out of doing those things. How to make it so that your clients understand the value you bring to their business and will be happy to pay for it.

First up — be public about your goals.

The first way to make that happen is to be up front about your goals — your commitment to making an impact.

We've always set what we call *Big Hairy and Audacious Goals,* giving ourselves outrageous, practically unattainable targets for the results we want to achieve for our clients. Once upon a time, we asked ourselves what would scare the pants off us in terms of setting an objective for tax savings for our clients. We settled on saving our clients $500,000 in tax *in the last 12 weeks of the financial year.* It seemed impossible, but we figured, if you're going to go, go big.

Long story short — we smashed that goal, and now we've accumulated over $10 million in tax savings for our clients. And we learned a spectacular life-lesson — if you set yourself *Big Hairy and Audacious Goals*, it motivates everyone around you to achieve them. It galvanises the clients and they're thrilled to be a part of it. And the sense of achievement, which the clients share, is an amazing motivator to go for the next BHaAG.

Watch the "SAVE $500K TAX' video on YouTube:

Celebrate your successes.

Of course, the way to prove what we'd done was to track every cent we saved, and make it public (just the dollar figure, not the clients involved or anything at all that might compromise their privacy of course).

When you enter the realm of being impact-driven and you're charging for the value you add to your client's business, it pays (literally!) to measure, track and chart the difference you make. You need to work with your clients to quantify the value you're bringing to their business, so they (and the world) can see what an impact you're having.

Meeting with your client to tell them that you've helped them bring in so many thousands of dollars of extra revenue, or saved them $xx,xxx in tax, or freed up their cashflow to the extent that they now have an extra $xx,xxx to spend or invest, you're achieving two things. First, you're getting the client excited about their business and showing them how much an investment in proactive, impact-driven accounting can pay off. And second, you're proving your individual contribution to their success.

So get tracking. Quantify the differences you make and make the most of them!

Impact statements — a powerful tool.

It's impossible to overstate the excitement and inspiration that takes over clients when you prove to them the difference your impact is making to their business. Sharing those moments with people is one of the great joys of being impact-driven. You just don't see that unbridled enthusiasm from people when you let them know you've lodged their BAS statement, or that their super payments are due.

So make a song and dance about it when you have good news to share. You already know about our Magic Number performance, but that's the tip of the iceberg. Whenever we have great news to thrill a client with, we ask them to make an Impact Statement. That's a simple piece of paper — laminated so it lasts — that outlines the Big Hairy and Audacious Goal at the top, with spaces for the client's name, business and of course a very large space for the Magic Number. At the bottom, we ask the question, *what are you going to do with your savings?* The answers range from the thoughtful — *I am going to reinvest in my business / I'm going to start a B1G1 project*, to the animated — *I plan to spend it on a family holiday / put it towards a new car*, to the downright hilarious. One of our favourite Impact Statements ever, because it made us laugh out loud, was simply *go on a bender.*

Back to U.

As I mentioned above, most of the items detailed in

R.E.S.U.L.T.S. above are part of your remit. You know that stuff, and you're damn good at it. So I won't presume to tell you any more about them.

The one issue that you may not know anything about, and which is vital to your future as an impact-driven business for good, is the U — UN Goals.. I say it's vital because to help you stand out in the world, you need to prove that you are committed to being a force for good. As Laurence Fink, the CEO of Blackrock said in 2007, "To prosper over time, every company must not only deliver financial performance, but also show how it makes a positive contribution to society."

About the Goals.

In September 2015, 193 countries signed the Un Global Goals for Sustainable Development. Pioneered by former Unilever CEO Paul Polman, the Goals are designed to "to promote prosperity while protecting the planet. They recognize that ending poverty must go hand-in-hand with strategies that build economic growth and address a range of social needs including education, health, social protection and job opportunities, while tackling climate change and environmental protection."

This wasn't the first time the UN had made public commitment to making a difference. In 2000, the organisation issued the Millennium Development Goals. Thanks to the success of that program, 43 million more kids go to school, new HIV infections decreased by 40%, and over 2 billion more people got clean drinking water. By 2015, extreme poverty had been halved.

We know that public declarations work, and they attract like-minded people eager to share in the attainment of the goals announced.

The Global Goals are the perfect starting point for incorporating giving into your business. I recommend checking out the list of Global Goals and finding one that resonates with your values. You can then use this as the catalyst for your first giving campaign.

Get involved.

Like all great *Big Hairy and Audacious Goals*, the UN Global Goals for Sustainable Development are backed by solid plans, and ways to get involved. You can download a toolkit to help you *Be the Change*, you can get ideas from the *Lazy Person's Guide to Saving the World*, and you can commit to the *170 Actions* that will help you make progress towards the *Global Goals*.

My hope is that one day all businesses will have the same attitude and adopt even more positive actions towards making our world a better place. But until that happens, committing to the UN Global Goals and taking other steps to being a business for good — more of which you'll learn in the next chapter — makes you stand out. In the meantime, any results you can achieve towards the UN Global Goals are worthwhile.

Outstanding results make you stand out.

Once again, we've covered a lot of varied ground in this chapter. The takeaway is that you have the skills and the experience to make an impact, and the results you achieve can make a real difference to your business, your clients and the world. So don't be shy about stating your *Big Hairy and Audacious Goals*, making commitments and following through, and measuring, tracking and sharing your successes.

The differences you make will astound and delight you and the momentum you gather will inspire your team, your clients and the people around you.

CHAPTER 8
I is for Improve our world.

Originally, we were going to call this chapter *I is for making an Impact*, but I changed my mind to use the current title: *I is for Improve the World*. Why? Because we've spoken a lot about impact and being impact-driven in this book so far, and I hope that by now you recognise that we're talking about a wide range of impacts — on your client's business, on your business and on making a positive contribution to the world.

But in this chapter, I want to focus on that last impact, making a positive contribution to the world. Going beyond the United Nations Global Goals for Sustainable Development and finding other ways of becoming a business for good. Improving our world. And if that isn't a *Big Hairy and Audacious Goal* I don't know what is.

So, you won the lottery.

Paul Polman, who we mentioned briefly in the previous chapter as the architect of the UN Global Goals for Sustainable Development, suggests that people like you and me are so fortunate because we have literally "won the lottery of birth." By virtue of where we were born and the opportunities afforded to us by that simple act of chance, we are among the lucky few who never have to worry too much about providing food, shelter, healthcare and education for our families.

Therefore it's on us, particularly in a world where there's a great deal of inequality and so many lack those privileges we're so used to that we regard them as rights, to share our good fortune. But in recent years, the realisation has dawned on many of us that helping people in far distant countries is not just about improving their lives, it's about making our world a more liveable, equitable and sustainable place. That's what the UN Global Goals are about after all — creating an environment in which all people and creatures, and indeed that environment itself, can not only survive but thrive.

As the saying goes, we do not inherit the world from our ancestors, we borrow it from our children.

WE DO NOT INHERIT THE WORLD FROM OUR ANCESTORS

WE BORROW IT FROM OUR CHILDREN

The challenge to business.

As part of this growing awareness of the fact that for the world to be a better place we all need to play our part in its improvement, in recent years there's also been a realisation that business has a pivotal and in fact a leading role to play in that improvement.

At the United Nations assembly back in 2015, when the Global Goals were adopted by 193 countries, it was said that governments don't change the world — the real change will be driven by business.

And when you think about it, that is so true. It almost doesn't matter what governments legislate or people march for, if business doesn't see a way forward in something, it will never gain any traction. That's just the way our world is and has been for a long time — society follows business, not the other way around, no matter how much we wish it wasn't the case.

So it makes sense that if we are going to create a more equitable, sustainable and liveable world, that change will be driven by business.

The good news? It's already happening.

There's a new phenomenon on the rise across the world, and it's called being a business for good. As we all know very well, business doesn't do anything just because it's good. It simply can't afford to. If it's not good for the business, then why would any business owner choose to do something that may be the end of their company? They wouldn't.

But it's now creeping into business consciousness around the world that having a purpose, doing good, can actually be good for business. Back to Paul Polman for a moment. Before he became famous for his UN initiative, Mr Polman was CEO of Unilever, one of the world's largest and most widespread companies. Mr Polman introduced a Sustainable Living Plan to his multi-billion-dollar corporation, an idea almost unthinkable at that time, and one which attracted a lot of cynicism and criticism. But he was right, and his idea helped Unilever to grow to new heights.

His story is well worth reading because of the traumatic experience that led to his awakening, but here's what he

181

had to say about creating a plan that went beyond the environment and into society itself: "So many companies with purpose are on the side of the environment which was very narrowly defined as trees and water and conservation. But it runs much deeper. We need to fight for addressing these issues of exclusion and poverty, which are at the roots of this violence. And so if you don't understand that human dimension, and that the crisis we face is one of humanity more so than anything else, you can't really properly solve it."

Unilever is one of the most famous examples of companies that found a purpose and have never looked back since. Here are just a few others:

ZAMBREROS

The mexican restaurant chain Zambreros has a 'Plate for Plate' campaign where for every burrito you buy, they give a meal to somebody in need. To date they've donated over 40 million meals to help end world hunger.

WHO GIVES A CRAP

There's an Australian toilet paper company called Who Gives A Crap who donate 50% of their profits to build toilets in the developing world. Their slogan is 'good for your bum and great for the world'.

GRILL'D BURGERS

When you buy a burger from Grill'd, you get a little token and you can choose from one of four causes to make a donation to. They give the consumer the choice of how they make an impact.

GOOD BEER CO

The Good Beer Co. is a social enterprise that exists to create and sell good beers to fund and support good causes. I love the guys of the good beer. You can buy Great Barrier Reef beer to support reef restoration, or Pale Tail to support the RSPCA.

WARBY PARKER

*Over in the United States, Warby Parker, who are kind of
like the Bailey Nielsen of Australia, do the 'buy a pair, give
a pair' campaign where for every pair of glasses you buy,
they give a pair of glasses to someone who needs them.*

**Buy A Pair,
Give A Pair**

For every pair purchased,
a pair is distributed to
someone in need

LEARN MORE

TOMS SHOES

TOMS shoes donate a pair of shoes to someone in a developing country every time you buy a pair of shoes.

These are great examples, but I'm not asking you to become Unilever or Zambreros. There are many, many companies around the world who don't get huge or famous, but who in ways big and small improve our world every day, and I want you to be one of those. You might not get the headlines, but you'll achieve a level of recognition that will surprise you, and it will act like a magnet drawing the right kind of clients to your business.

I'll provide you with more detail on how fast and easy it is to become a business for good shortly, with a few simple actions that set you on the path to making a global impact. But first, a word or two about our business and the unique position you're in.

Maybe your purpose is to spread the idea of purpose.

You spend your days helping business owners grow, streamline and advance their businesses. You have a unique insight into the minds and lives of your clients as well as their businesses, and you're closer than almost anyone else to what their purpose is.

That puts you in the best possible position to speak to your clients about being a business with purpose, articulating the benefits of taking up that purpose, and helping them achieve their goals in that direction. You can use your experience — and your successes in attaining goals and making impacts — to prove to them that the concept works.

You can be an agent of change, multiplying the good that your business is already adding to the world.

The benefits of being a business for good.

Time and time again, businesses have proven that rather than being a cost, becoming a force for good has a positive effect on the bottom line, and a range of other aspects of the business.

The subtitle of this book is *Become the STANDOUT accounting firm that people want to buy from, work for and rave about*, and that's an accurate description of some of the benefits of becoming a business for good.

It starts with clients coming to you because they see the good you're doing, the improvements you're making to the world, and they want to take advantage of your experience to do the same. Your approach becomes a magnet for people who want to emulate your ways and become a force for good themselves. That means you're attracting clients who think the way you do and who share your values. It's a match made in heaven.

Of course, clients like that will rave about you, especially when they begin to see the effects of becoming a force for good on their businesses. It's natural that they will talk about this seismic change in their lives and do their best to convince others to experience that change themselves. It's a beautiful and self-sustaining referral mechanism.

But one of the biggest changes you'll see is in your staff. Having a purpose works a magical change in people and makes them so much happier, engaged and productive. As Cynthia Bell writes in the Deloitte 2020 Trends Report, "Purpose matters to employees too. People want to find meaning in their work, so they're attracted to companies with purpose and are three times more likely to stay there."

Our experience backs this up — our team members are actually pumped about coming to work, and as we near each new goal they become more animated, more enthusiastic and more dedicated to making it happen. It really is remarkable.

A little backstory.

A few years ago, we were invited to spend a week on Sir Richard Branson's Necker Island in the British Virgin Islands. What an honour, to spend time with a group of heavy hitters, talking about how we could improve our earth. Imagine the conversations we could have and the connections we could make!

But at about the same time, some sad and difficult statistics came to our attention. We found out that across this world, 663 million people live without access to clean drinking water. Every. Single. Day.

Instead of spending the money to fly to Necker Island, which would have been an amazing experience, we elected to instead do something practical. We turned our attention to Malawi, a tiny country in Africa with around 20 million people, 1.6 million of whom were living, and in many cases dying, without access to clean drinking water.

1 Million Days.

Watch #GIVE1MDAYS video on YouTube

That was the moment we decided to launch our 1 Million Days campaign. For every dollar of tax we saved for our clients, we would donate one day of access to clean drinking water. To achieve this goal, we would need to proactively save our clients $1 million in tax. So we set the goal and got to work. We promised to hit the ground in Malawi once we reached our goal, to show our clients firsthand the impact we were making.

We started to integrate giving into little impacts that we had in our business and that really gave birth to the now famous giving initiative — Day for a Dollar. We give a day of access to food, water, health, and sanitation to a family in need, for every dollar of tax that we proactively save our small business clients.

The campaign far exceeded our expectations. As of January 2020, the team had proactively saved its clients over ten million dollars in tax, and thanks to our day for a dollar initiative, we've also given over ten million days of life-changing help to families in need in over 16 countries.

The impact of that decision not to go to Necker Island has been indescribable. Giving ten million days of life-giving help to people all over the world has been a humbling, gratifying and empowering experience that I wish everyone I meet could share. But the impact spreads beyond the good we do for the people in those faraway places who've never even heard of us.

The team is incredibly motivated to keep going, to improve our reach and the multiply the good we do. And the only way we get to do that good is to keep on saving money for our clients — so you can imagine just how enthusiastic and supportive they are of our goals. Every time we announce a new goal, our clients realise that they're going to share in the impact we create, so they're right behind us all the way.

We never lose sight of the fact that our purpose is to improve the world, but we don't shy away from the fact that while we are doing good for the world, we are also creating a positive impact for our teams and their families, our clients and their families, and contributing to the success of our economy.

Once you get involved in something this life-changing, it becomes addictive. You want to do more good, and the way to facilitate that is to do more good for your clients. It's a self-reinforcing positive cycle that we're happy to be embedded in.

Our Holiday for Good

In 2018, my fiancée (now my wife) and I took my daughter and one of my nephews on a Holiday for Good to Cambodia. We wanted to see firsthand some of the impact that we were making through this giving initiative.

I wanted to show the kids that they kind of already lived in Disneyland, and to help them gain an appreciation for how lucky they are to be born in Australia. Cambodia is a beautiful country filled with absolutely wonderful, friendly and welcoming people who endure some of the worst poverty in Southeast Asia. Their history is traumatic, and there are still many people alive there who lived through the dark days of the Pol Pot regime — a time when up to 20% of the Cambodian population died at the dictator's hands.

We visited some of these families and saw the conditions in which they live, and I took one photo that blew my mind. These poor kids were living in conditions that we probably wouldn't even let our pets live in, and I took a photo of my 10-year-old nephew, Ruben with a local Cambodian boy who was also 10. The difference was stark. Ruben was almost twice his size. It was hard to believe they were the same age.

I look at this photo often and I think about the injustice of what's out there in the world and this crazy idea that one of these boys won the human lottery just by being born in Australia.

This is why we commit to improving our world. So that kids like that cheerful but terribly underprivileged kid in Cambodia can have the kind of food, shelter and education we take for granted.

It's your turn now.

As you can probably tell, my adventures in improving the world are amazing, and I could go on about them forever. It's so fulfilling to make an impact like that. And it's so encouraging to find that clients are super keen to work with us when they find out how much good we can do with them and on their behalf, as well as for them.

There are a number of ways you can get involved in improving our world and the lives of the people who share it. We've already spoken about the UN Global Goals for Sustainable Development, and I again urge you to commit to one or more of the goals and play your part in achieving them.

But there are other things you can do to help improve our world, and I'll talk about a couple of them briefly now. If you want to know more, you can read my book *Become a Business for Good*, which provides much more detail.

B1G1 — Buy 1 Give 1

This brilliant initiative is something we've been part of for quite some time now, and we just love how easy and effective it is. The idea is straightforward — you just keep doing what you're doing, and when a certain action or milestone happens in your business, you give.

The most recognisable example is, say you own a coffee shop. Every time you sell a coffee, you can choose to make a gift. It could be giving seeds to help nourish a child in Kenya for one cent per cup, or give access to water to a family in Cambodia for nine cents a cup.

There are hundreds and hundreds of giving opportunities

across categories like Food, Health, Environment, Education and Human Rights, and the prices range from less than a cent to thousands of dollars.

As an accountant, you might say to yourself that every time you complete an income tax return you'll give $5 to provide a meal for a rescued girl in India, or $10 to provide business training to women in Guatemala. Or you might say, for every ten thousand dollars you save your clients collectively, you'll employ a doctor in Kenya for $590, or provide a safe home for sexually abused children in Nepal for $1569.

As you know, every time we save our clients a dollar in tax, we give access to drinking water or food, so you could easily structure your giving around the goals you have for saving your clients money, improving their revenue or cashflow or whatever.

The great thing about B1G1 is that your giving is automatically tracked via an interactive world map. You can add a widget to your website so that all visitors can see exactly what you're giving and where, or take snapshots and put them in emails, print them for your boardroom, or make any use you like of them.

You can also change what you give in just a few minutes, so that your giving is always dynamic and visible.

It's fast, easy and free to sign up for B1G1, and it gives you a platform for giving that's trackable and well-accounted for — and you'll be joining thousands of businesses from around the world who are making their own differences through it. And once your clients see what an improvement you're making to the world, I guarantee they'll be interested in doing the same — at least the ones worth keeping as clients will be.

Become a B Corp.

When you're ready to be a force for good, you can publicly commit to living by your values by becoming a B Corporation. As their website says, "Certified B Corporations are businesses that meet the highest standards of verified social and environmental performance, public transparency, and legal accountability to balance profit and purpose."

It takes a bit more work and some costs to certify as a B Corp, but along the way you'll learn what the organisation is all about, and how it helps to improve our world. The basics are that the enlisted companies work to achieve behavioural and social shifts across 5 different areas:

1. Industry Shift

2. Urban Shift

3. Energy Shift

4. Land Shift

5. Cultural Shift

Even if all the levers aren't directly relatable to accountants, it's valuable to understand and participate in B Corp because it gives you the tools to help your clients become involved. Investigate B Corp and consider joining companies like Patagonia, Beyond Bank, Aesop Cosmetics, T2 Tea and Atticus Health.

It all comes back to your values.

#Inspo: Here's an example of the philosophy stickers I created to make our brand come alive.

This book is about becoming a Stand Out accountant, and making the decision to contribute to improving the world is a huge step in that direction. Being a business that gives, changes your perspective and your focus, and reminds all your stakeholders — your business owners, your team, your clients and the people around you — what's really important.

It also gives you a genuine point of difference that has a real meaning to the clients considering working with you. It takes you out of the realm of the typical accountant and into an orbit where you're active, caring, mindful and impactful.

I can personally vouch for the positive effect that being a business for good will bring to your life, and I'm always happy to share more of my experiences. If you want to know more, ask me.

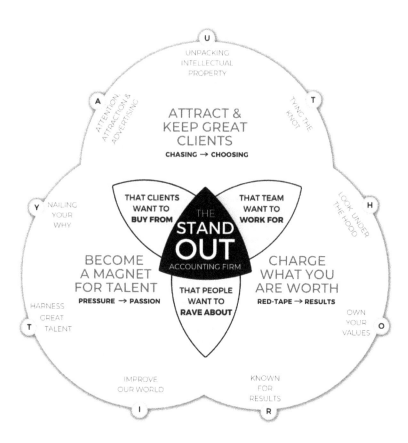

CHAPTER 9
T is for the Talent you'll attract.

Throughout this book we've concentrated on the ways you can run your business and create impacts to become a business for good, primarily with an eye to attracting clients — the people who will buy from and rave about you. But what about the people who, seeing the way you run your business, will want to work for you.

I confess, although they merit a third of the subtitle, in some ways I've neglected this group so far. Although in my defence, I have made it clear that every time you set or achieve a goal, whether client or global impact-oriented, it has an enormous positive effect on your team.

But in this chapter, we'll look at how you can ensure that you attract the right people, how you know you have and how to retain them. When you become a business for good, the team members you have now will be more likely to stay with you, and you'll be more likely to become an employer of choice. That means people in the industry will look for ways to come and work with you. So the trick will not really be in attracting talent, but choosing which of the applicants fits your ethos and ensuring they understand and agree with what they're buying into.

We'll get started in a second, but first I want to tell a story that illustrates the kind of people you want to have on board. It's all about subtle mind shifts that make a tremendous difference.

Laying bricks or building a cathedral...

A traveller encountered three men working on a huge building site. He asked the first man what he was doing, and the man said he was laying bricks. He asked the second man the same question and he said he was putting up a wall. When he got to the third man and asked him what he was doing the third man said, "I'm building a cathedral."

They were all doing the same thing, but the first man had a job, the second man had a career…and the third man had a calling.

The point being, of course, that you want that third bricklayer working for you. Sure, the others may be adequate brickies, but the one that I would hire is always the one that shares the vision.

The other point is, it's okay to exercise discernment when you're hiring. Choose the people that honestly share your vision and aren't afraid to say it out loud. You're going to be spending a lot of time with these people, so you want to be damn sure they're going to fit in, that they're going to do a great job and that they're going to be awesome ambassadors for your business.

Choosing the right people.

Not everyone will be right for your team. That's a given. But how can you be sure you're selecting the right applicants? Some of the people who want to come and work with you will be attracted by the idea of getting more money for the same work done differently. Some will be attracted by the fame or reputation of your business. But the ones you really want are the ones that are drawn to you because of the impacts you make.

Obviously, the ones that say all the right things in the interviews about being impact-driven and sharing your vision will be the front runners. But we apply a final test of sorts. We give them our *Human Code of Conduct* document and let them know that if they agree to abide by the terms the rest of the team lives by, they're a good fit. If not, well, no hard feelings.

Our Human Code of Conduct

I'll just leave these here without any comment — but put yourself in the place of a shortlisted candidate who's seeing these for the first time and being asked to commit to them. As we always say, it's not for everyone...:

Agreement 1 — Marathons & Sprint

Marathons & Sprints

Like Dog Years, a single year at Inspire could be likened to seven years in a more traditional firm. We run at a serious pace. To avoid burnout, we run our business to a "3 x 4" rhythm or 3 x 4 month quarters in a year instead of the traditional "4 x 3". Each quarter will have a clear theme and focus, and every team member will know their role to play, climaxing with a month of celebration.

Agreement 2 — Sharpening the Axe

Sharpening the Axe

Celebration months are a great opportunity for 'Service and Maintenance' as it's the only time that 'the speed train' — that is Inspire — slows down long enough to onboard new team members or to allow team members to take a well earned holiday or do some epic personal and professional development. In November, March and July each year for example, we celebrate our wins with a 2-day offsite team retreat called Thinking and Thanking Day.

Agreement 3 — The Game Plan

The Game Plan

*Like a team in a locker room moments before running onto the field, our Thinking & Thanking Day team retreats help every person on the team know exactly the role they each play in winning the game. Client Service Coordinators, Account Managers, Business Development Managers and Quality Controllers, each have a different (but complementary) role to play for the quarter, summarised in one key Measure of Success. For example, "5 x Proactive Advice Meetings / week" or "5 x 2nd Opinions on Tax / week" when repeated 13 times over the 13 weeks in a quarter keeps us each 'on track' to win as a team. Because we are all dependant on each other, it's fine to be ahead, or on track but **it is not ok to be behind.***

Agreement 4 — Own the Day

Own the Day

To help you create space for personal or family success, we do an 'early start, early finish' with office hours between 7:20 and 3:50. Daily at 7:47 sharp (yes, that 'sharp') we assemble in a circle for a Standing Team Huddle where we each share 3 things — What am I grateful for? What are my top 3 priorities for today? Am I ahead, on track or behind with my Measures of Success?

Think of "747" as everyone standing around a campfire and the goal is to get everyone warmed up. What you say and how you say it can be like either throwing cold water or fuel on the fire. Please be brief, inspirational and to the point.

Agreement 5 — Get Stuff Done

Get Stuff Done

Ever noticed how productive you are when you've worked either on an airplane, from home or at a cafe with your headphones on? Distractions are the enemy of productivity. That's why "747" is followed by 2 hours of GSD time — no emails, no client meetings, no phone calls and best of all, no one tapping you on the shoulder to ask a question, until 10 a.m. Seriously, unless there's a comet about to hit our office, don't bug anyone.

Agreement 6 — Batch Sh*t Crazy

*Batch Sh*t Crazy*

The relentless pursuit of GSD also sees us 'batch' all our client meetings on Tuesday — Thursday, leaving Monday's & Friday's to prepare and follow up. It's also why we don't live in our inboxes. Emails are only 'let in' to our inbox 3 times a day — thanks to some software called Boomerang.

Agreement 7 — Inbox Zero

Inbox Zero

Every day we achieve Inbox Zero. Every email in our inbox is either acknowledged or actioned on the day it's received. Most client emails are actually answered by our team of Client Service Coordinators and Junior Accountants. So it's just the curly ones that make it through to you. Inbox Zero helps us stay well within our promise to our clients of a "guaranteed 24-hour response to your questions, or we'll send you something great".

Agreement 8 — Gratitude is a Game Changer

Gratitude is a Game Changer

Every Friday morning we do Team Thankyou. It's a standing circle of gratitude where we THANK each other for the impact we've heard or seen each other make during the week. There's laughter, there's smiles and sometimes even tears. Definitely the highlight of the week.

Agreement 9 — Deadlines Become Lifelines

Deadlines Become Lifelines

Preparing Tax Returns and Financial Statements is like driving in a car looking through the rear vision mirror. While being compliant with the authorities is important, we ultimately want Inspire clients to make the 7 Smart Financial Decisions of a Cashed Up business. That's why we turn Tax Office Deadlines into Business Lifelines through early lodgment and proactive advice — this is like looking through the front windscreen, helping clients take the shortest and fastest route to their destination. For example —

- *Quarterly BAS (a Business Activity Statement required by the Government every quarter in Australia) are finalised 2 weeks before they're due, so clients have time to plan cashflow.*
- *Tax Planning is done with every client by May 15, so clients still have 6 weeks to implement before 30 June.*
- *We run an 'Annual General Meeting' with each client when we finish their Tax Returns and Financial Statements in October, so they still have Nov — June to make this the best financial year yet.*

Agreement 10 — Death Before Timesheets

Death Before Timesheets

You may know by now we don't do timesheets. So ... what do we measure then?

Just one thing: Impact.

- *Tax Savings*
- *Increases in Profit & Business Value & Wealth*
- *Reduction in Cashflow Days, Debt & Cost of Living.*
- *The ultimate impact is Freedom Days. It's calculated by "Net Wealth / Cost of Living per Day" and is really the sum of all these impacts combined.*

At Inspire we believe that 'Advice Precedes Impact'. Instead of timesheets, every day and every week we track the number of "Proactive Advice Meetings" we've delivered, then every quarter we measure the impact of our advice on our clients' business and lives.

Agreement 11 — Communication over Calculation

Communication over Calculation

He who communicates best wins. To date, your career progression has been focused around upping your technical knowledge. From here on in it's about becoming a MASTER COMMUNICATOR. Knowing your stuff is important, but that just gets you a foot in the door. "Making an impact", becoming a "Life-Changing Accountant" and helping people get "Cashed Up" requires you to learn how to communicate in such a way that people listen, take action and leave feeling inspired.

Agreement 12 — Dress to Impress

Dress to Impress

*The dress code at Inspire is Super Smart Casual. We want to strike the fine balance between "I'm down to earth and approachable" and "I'm a qualified professional, ready to make an impact". You'll **never** see us in a suit or tie. Some cool jeans or a skirt with an Inspire T Shirt and a collared shirt over the top will do the trick. In short, we want people to judge us by the impact we make, not the clothes we wear. However we'd never want to dress in such a way that people find it hard to have instant trust in sharing with us their most intimate financial details.*

Agreement 13 — Leave, Leave, Leave

Leave, Leave, Leave

Annual Leave ...

Celebration months are a great time to take leave, but you're free to take annual leave whenever you like (as long as you give plenty of notice)! Just put your initials on the dates you're thinking of taking in the Activities Calendar. At our Quarterly Retreats we help you to plan your holidays a year in advance so you always have something to look forward to.

Sick Leave ...

If you're sick, you're sick. Just take the day off and get better. We'll see you again the next day when you're 100%. Your emails and client meetings will still be there for you when you get back. No need to work from home.

I'm-not-really-feeling-it-so-I'm-working-from-home-or-leaving-early-leave ...

We're definitely not a team of clock-watchers, but out of respect for the team we're all part of, we show up on time and ready to make an impact. We don't duck off early and there's not really a culture of working from home. We recognise that we're part of an inspirational team of game changers and we value the opportunity we have to work side-by-side with people we actually respect (and even love).

Agreement 14 — High-five the status quo in the face — with a chair

> **High-five the status quo in the face — with a chair**
>
> *We are best selling authors. We've won multiple awards. We regularly get invited to feature in the media and speak on business and personal success around Australia and internationally. Although we've just begun, we believe that we are already worthy of the title 'Australia's Most Impactful Accounting Firm." That simply is not possible without a culture of extreme innovation, profound rejection of the status quo and a strong desire for everyone to embrace change.* **You up for the challenge?**

Over to you.

I'm not suggesting you copy the 14 agreements word for word. Although imitation is the sincerest form of flattery, I'm sure you'd rather come up with your own ways of marshalling and rewarding the talent you attract. Just be sure and put it all on paper and use it to vet the applicants you get when your business expands through the impacts you make.

Rituals

One of the actions we find most successful in bringing and keeping the team together, and keeping our collective eyes on the prize, is to regularly schedule meetings and get togethers that function as reminders, motivators and rewards in fun settings.

Tristan White from The Physio Co (eight times ranked *Australia's Best Place to Work)* describes a daily huddle as a bit like a time-out in a basketball game. "The team comes together for a short time to discuss the next move. In basketball, that means deciding who will do what and when — each player has a role to fill — and then the team leaves the huddle with an extra oomph of energy."

The Inspire team has an 'early start, early finish' office hours schedule starting at 7:20 and ending 3:50 to help create space for personal and/or family success. With such an early start, we wanted to create a way of kicking off the day with that bit of 'extra oomph'.

747

At 7:45 Alexa (our voice-activated speaker) plays the theme song from *The Lion King* — you know the one 'naaaahhhhhh-nawhen-yaaaah' — which lets everyone know it's time for 747.

Everyone gets out of their chairs and taps a colleague on the shoulder as they make their way down to our team Huddle Space to form a standing circle.

One wall of the Huddle Space is covered with hundreds of

Impact Statements — full of the feelings of happy clients, their tax savings and what a difference it's making to their life. On another wall are some of the philosophies in big black frames — "I had too much to dream last night", "Accountants Change Lives", "Businesses Who Do Good Do Better."

On the third wall is a massive 3 x 3 m blackboard that has all the key performance indicators for the whole team listed — the quarterly theme, number of leads, % completion of the required Quarterly Business Activity Statements (BAS) for clients, Year End data, New Client meetings.

Turning to the final 4th wall you see a massive one-page game plan that includes the 10 year, 3 year, annual and quarterly goals alongside our vision, mission and values. Having the *One Page Game Plan* visible to everyone in the team keeps everyone accountable to the idea that we all have different roles to play on the field and we can only win as a team by playing together.

By 7:47 the song finishes and the 'Huddle Master' for that week begins with a one-minute icebreaker — perhaps a joke, an inspirational quote, a stretch of the body, a thought for the day. Then everyone each reads a sentence (working the way around the circle until done) on the *Daily Standing Huddle Opener:*

DAILY STANDING HUDDLE

Welcome to 747 — allow me to kick off this standing team huddle by reminding us all of some key principles —

Today is a new day.

And with it comes a new opportunity to —

Dream Big. Make an Impact. Remember Your Roots.

May I remind you of our mission —

To become, **"Australia's Most Impactful Accounting Firm".**

Whether it's the tax we save a **family,**

on the other side of the desk.

Or the life-changing help we give a **family,**

on the other side of the world.

We believe and we know that **Accountants Change Lives.**

And today is another opportunity to do just that.

We know that **"Advice Precedes Impact"**

So let's be **proactive** *today in the advice we give.*

747 is a chance to come together as a team.

To get focus on just 3 things.

What are we grateful for?

What are our top 3 priorities for the day?

Do we need a hand?

Let's keep it brief. **Inspirational.** *To the point.*

[Name] let's start with you...

So let's break down the key ingredients...

Standing

The Daily Huddle is about lifting energy and gaining focus. Standing gets our blood flowing, changes our state and physiologically gets us looking up — perfect for a huddle.

Timing

Choosing a strange time that stands out means everyone respects it. That's one reason why you'll notice that planes take off at 'strange' times — 10:03, 3:18, 11:47. At our place, 7:47 means 7:47 not 7:49 or 7:51.

The Huddle is ingrained in me now. It's been one of the most valuable rituals the team created and had the discipline to stick to. Improvements in teamwork, communication, accountability, energy, growth and profit have all occurred since starting a huddle.

Endings are as important as beginnings.

Have you ever finished a big project or a big day or week where you've ticked lots of boxes and achieved lots of things but still feel a little bit empty inside?

The daily standing Huddle is a great way to lift productivity and achievement, but it isn't quite enough. There is one more thing we'd love you to have as a ritual too.

It's a weekly *Thank You Circle*. It's inspired by a ritual from the team at Thankyou HQ (a Social Enterprise where 100% of the profits go towards ending extreme global poverty).

Every Friday morning, we do Team Thank You — a standing circle of gratitude where we thank each other for the impact we've heard or seen each other make during the week.

Team Thank You gives you a wonderful platform as a leader to acknowledge people publicly for the impact they've made. Imagine you wanted to thank 'Johnny' for great work on a client project. You could thank Johnny via an email or a text message or one on one in your office, but take that same acknowledgement (the message) and deliver that to Johnny publicly in front of all his peers, followed by applause (the setting) and Johnny will have a very, very powerful experience.

We found that as soon as we implemented the Weekly Thank You Circle almost all remnants of BS, drama and politics disappeared. Once you're standing in a small intimate circle of close peers for 30 minutes to an hour each week covering each other in praise and acknowledgement for the impact they've made, it's very difficult to harbour animosity, resentment or feelings of being unappreciated.

Of course, like all great rituals, there is a structure to it ....

WEEKLY GRATITUDE CIRCLE

Welcome to our weekly Thank You Circle. Allow me to kick off this standing team gratitude circle by reminding us all of some key principles —

One of the most powerful words we can say is "Thank you", because gratitude is the great multiplier.

Be thankful for what you do have in your life, and you tend to get more of it.

In reverse, complain about what you don't have in life, and you tend to get less of it.

How Team Thankyou works is we gather around in a circle and thank each other for the impact you've seen (or heard) someone make in the last week.

For example -

"Ethan I want to Thank You for coming around and cleaning up the bins and everyone's workstations. It really made for a fresh working environment and it made my life easier. Thank You."

"Kathryn I want to thank you for proactively calling the Australian Tax Office and negotiating the penalties and interest remission for the Greer Family Trust. They really appreciated it and were so surprised with the 'out of the blue' refund."

Team Thank You is the one time each week that we step aside from the busy-ness that is Inspire, and remind ourselves of the impact we've each made and how grateful we are to be surrounded by people who inspire us.

The idea is we never ever leave a Thank You circle without feeling acknowledged and appreciated for the impact we've made. There's no order or time limit. "So [Name] would you like to kick us off?"

Team Thank You is the one time each week that we step aside from the busy-ness and remind ourselves of the impact we'vc each made and how grateful we are to be surrounded by people who inspire us.

The idea is we never ever leave a Thank You circle without feeling acknowledged and appreciated for the impact we've made.

One more thought.

Throughout this book, we've harped on the idea of creating a firm to which people want to belong. So... here's the extra thought... what if you could involve your customers (clients) in the Thank You Friday too? Here's how you might do that and create an extra spirit of giving too using the power of B1G1.

All you have to do is add a little piece to the Thank You Circle where you actually 'call out' your clients (it could be new clients who've joined, clients who've referred others, people who paid their bills on time and so on) to thank them for all they've done this week.

Here's what it might look like in a thank you note to the client(s):

Hello <client first name>,

If your ears were burning today, I want to explain why.

Every week here at <name of firm> we have a Thankyou Circle where we specifically express our gratitude in great ways to our fellow Team Members who've done great things during the week.

And it may surprise you to know <client first name> that we also took some time this week to thank the clients who joined us this week, including you. And that's why your ears were burning!

To make sure we really do celebrate that, we always do a special giving through B1G1. This week, <Team Member name> was the one who was in charge of choosing the giving.

Here's the outcome: as a result of new clients coming on board this week, we've given 103 days of game-changing e-learning education to children in need.

So, <client first name>, THANK YOU.

The wind up.

As a business driven by impact, and being a force for good, your firm will be a place where people want to work. Like your clients, they'll rave about you and encourage their friends to join in.

Creating the human terms, the rituals and the environment that will make your team members feel valued, empowered and motivated will help to ensure that they remain productive and committed to your business, your cause and their own goals.

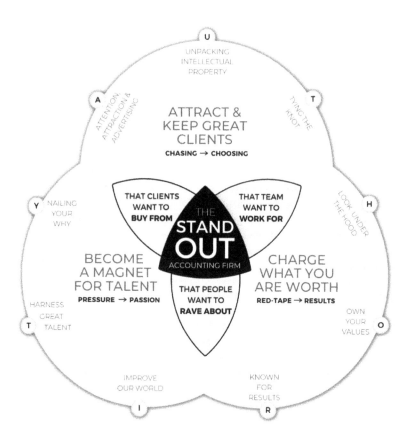

CHAPTER 10
Y is for Nailing your Why.

Mark Twain said it well when he wrote, "The two most important days of your life are the day you're born and the day you find out why."

I was, in an odd sense, "lucky". The day I found out why I was put on this earth was the day I lay on an operating table with a surgeon about to excise a lump off my left testicle. I had a million things racing through my mind at that point, but the one question that kept repeating over and over again in my head was, *'If this is the last day of my life, can I be happy with what I'm leaving behind?'*

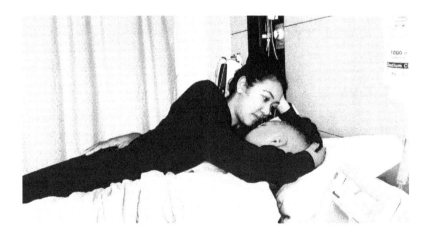

Right then and there, I found my purpose, and that — assuming I would survive — would be to do good and inspire others to do good.

As it happened, I not only survived that day, but I also beat the cancer in my system and I embarked on a mission to be true to the purpose that I'd discovered. And that led to a whole series of other seriously great moments. One of them is writing this book and making it as inspiring as I can for you.

But I don't want this book to be my story — I want it to be yours. I want you to use the insights and the examples to craft your own *why* and everything that springs from that. Like, for example, creating an accounting firm that inspires you and everyone in it.

And just consider for a moment the likely impact of that on your community, on your clients and, as you'll see, on our world.

The power of purpose.

The power of purpose is similar to the energy of sunlight focused through a magnifying glass. Sunlight may keep you warm or bring the colours to the grass, the sky and the people around you, but when that same energy is concentrated through a magnifying glass it can set fire to paper. Focus its energy even more, think laser beam, and it has the power to cut through steel.

In the same way, **a clear sense of purpose enables you to focus your efforts on what matters most, compelling you to take risks and to push forward regardless of the odds or obstacles.**

When you know your *why* your *what* has so much more power.

So, it's critical in your journey to becoming a Stand Out accountant that you find your personal *why* — because only then can you express that in your business.

Have you found your why?

It may be that you have already found your why, or what you believe it to be. You may have formulated a mission along the lines of "to be the best darn accountant I can be, by being diligent, conscientious and attentive to my clients' needs." But that, my friend, is a *what* and a *how*, not a *why*. And the world is full of people who can do exactly those things.

As Simon Sinek, the man behind 'Start with Why' says, "People don't buy what you do, they buy why you do it."

That makes *why* an emotional question. You need to get an emotional response yourself when you discover and articulate your *why*, and you need to see people smile and nod enthusiastically when you tell them. Picture yourself at an event, and when someone says, "what do you do?", instead of the same old, "oh, I'm an accountant," say something like, "I change the world and make my community a better place, one tax return at a time," or something like that. What sort of a reaction would you get?

How to find your purpose.

That said, you can't just make up a purpose. You have to feel it in your heart. At a recent webinar, Paul Dunn, Chairman of Buy1Give1 was discussing Purpose. One of the exercises he suggested the participants try was related to articulating our Purpose, defining our *Why*. It's a very simple process, like many of the best ideas are, so I thought I'd share this with you:

Find a quiet room (or a noisy one if you prefer), and using the voice recorder on your phone, complete this sentence...

"I get up every morning to............"

Why use a recording and not just write it down?

I know I'm never very keen to hear my own voice but when we write we tend to use words that aren't naturally ours, in that split-second delay between brain and hand we start to judge and amend the content. However, the spoken word tends to be more genuine and flows more naturally.

Your first recording will probably be something like: "I get up every morning to err um, oh no that sounds rubbish....... where's the off button?!"

Don't worry, just start again and record as many times as you need.

Listen back to your recording. How does it sound? And I'm referring to the content, not your voice.

Think about saying this to a potential client or at a networking meeting, what sort of response do you think you'd get?

When we consider our sentence from a potential client's perspective we may find that the sentence is rather focused on just us and could evoke a "that's nice but so what type of response!" Your Purpose is bigger than just the impact on you, so try the recording again including the two words

231

....so that....

"I get up every morning to.............. so that............................"

The inclusion of two simple words moves the sentence on, from just being just about you to a wider level of engagement.

For some, this exercise can be a real challenge, the concept of Purpose is just too big or far removed from today. Some feel as though they are defining their lifelong purpose, their life legacy and it's just too much, if that's the case, add the words

For now,........

For now, I get up every morning to......................so that..................

Another route to the truth.

That way doesn't work for everyone, so here's another. Kerwin Rae talks about the idea that every organism, whether it's an ant or a single-cell bacteria, has a purpose, and the more connected it is with the purpose the more efficient and effective its life is.

Humans, however, aren't born with an obvious purpose, so we could say that the purpose of our life is to find the purpose of life.

So here are nine questions that may well help you unearth your purpose:

1. What do you enjoy reading about?

2. What do you talk most passionately about?

3. What do you fantasise about?

4. What do you do in your spare time?

5. When are you lost in time and space?

6. When are you in flow?

7. What do you love?

8. What are you so passionate about that you'd do it every single day without pay?

9. What do you think you were put on this earth to do?

An Inspire-ing story.

If you're not getting any closer to nailing your *Why*, maybe this story will help.

When I first joined Inspire, we were a three-and-a-half-man band struggling to get any real traction. We worked long hours, took no holidays and lived up to the most common perception of accountants — boring.

When we were asked "What do you do?", the best answer we could summon at the time was "We do tax!" This was really frustrating because we had a big vision to create an accounting firm that redefined what was possible in a very traditional and very competitive industry, but we didn't articulate that.

With 12,000 other accounting firms in Australia (aka 'competitors') and the average age of an accounting firm owner at 58, we felt paralysed by the fact that all our competitors had more life experience, more technical experience, larger teams, fancier offices and bigger marketing budgets.

That was until we realised that we weren't actually in the business of Tax & Accounting, so the truth was we didn't have to compete with those older and wiser heads who were. No, we decided we were in the business of:

- Getting Cashed Up.

- Smart Financial Decisions.

- Pulling More Money, Time and Happiness from Your Business.

- Putting Family First.

- Business for Good and

- Making a difference in the lives of people we'll never get to meet.

The moment we shifted into that mindset, everything changed — our team, our culture, our thinking and how we showed up in the world. — And the world started to listen.

That's the power of a compelling answer to 'What do you do?'

How our core purpose evolved over time.

"We're numbers people and we believe that family is number one" was our first powerful realisation. So from that point on, 'Young Families' became central to our target market and therefore our social pitch.

Before: *We'll get your tax done!*

After: *We help Young Families use their Small Business to Achieve Big Goals.*

Then, our mentor Glen Carlson kept saying "if you think it's about tax and accounting you've missed the point!". And he was right … once we realised that we were in the business of *Impact, Money, Time and Happiness, Smart Financial Decisions, Doing Good* and the rest, we stumbled across our prize: **Cashed Up**. That simple phrase became part of our social pitch and the title of our book, a seven step methodology, our workshop themes and scorecard.

Before: *We help Young Families use their Small Business to Achieve Big Goals.*

After: *We help Young Families use their Small Business to get Cashed Up.*

Finally, once the *Cashed Up* book was published and we had pitched our *Cashed Up* methodology about 1,000 times, we noticed something amazing happening with our business clients. Many were so inspired by our *Business for Good* philosophies and the *Day for Dollar* giving initiative that as we helped them to save tax, boost profits and accelerate cashflow, they started embedding giving into their business too, becoming *Businesses for Good*. And so was born, the *Inspiring Business for Good Podcast* and the final tweak to our pitch -

Get Cashed Up >>> *We help Young Families get Cashed Up, so they can use their Business for Good.*

The *Inspiring Business for Good Podcast* debuted in the Top 100 in Australia on iTunes (in the category of Business News) and has been there ever since. On it we've been able to showcase our best clients, demonstrating how businesses can exist for good — for the good of their founders, their team, their clients and the world. The podcast has even inspired my next book *Doing Good is the New Great*.

Purpose + Values.

My mentor Jack Delosa describes *Values* as how we *"bottle the magic that was captured in the early years. It is how we put language to the previously unspoken. It is how we articulate what most never voice. Values should not be a list of principles that we 'create' and put over a business, but rather a set of principles that are actually discovered already lying deep within the existing DNA of the business."*

Bottling the magic.

To discover our Core Values, I took a two-week break from work and reflected on what was important to us and how those behaviours could be documented and demonstrated in a clear and inspiring way.

It's important to note that our core values were discovered, not created.

The behaviours and beliefs underpinning how our team act were already understood — we had all, to an extent, internalised them. It was the documenting of these beliefs into actionable words that had been the missing step. The core values took a long time to craft — like our core purpose. I discussed many drafts with a small number of teammates before I felt we had arrived at the right words.

Our Core Values.

Each core value is a principle accompanied by more detailed behaviours that exemplify that value in action. The beauty of this is that the detail reveals exactly what we expect of ourselves and our fellow team members.

The core values are:

- **Dream Big**

- **Make an Impact**

- **Remember your roots**

Every day we work to achieve our goals by consistently living our values. Any decision, problem or issue can be answered by referring to them. As with our core purpose, I repeat our core values frequently in conversations, meetings and interviews.

To give you a better sense of why core values are important for your business, let me run you through the behaviours attached and how we live them every day in every interaction with people.

Dream Big.

'Dream Big', is about showing up and challenging yourself and others to greatness. This means we shoot for the moon, challenge ourselves and others to greatness, step outside our comfort zone and take risks, be creative, and step up and get better.

Make an Impact.

Inspired by the late Steve Jobs famous quote that said, "We're here to make a dent in the universe, otherwise why else even be here?". This means:

- We're here to GSD or "get sh*t done".

- Make an impact and get results.

- Do meaningful work — you're not here to look good and go nowhere.

- Fulfil business and personal potential — be productive in all you do.

Remember your roots

Always maintain a strong connection to what grounds you — your motivation: your *why*. Your *why* anchors you to the reason you are on this planet, why you get out of bed in the morning and why you do your life's best work every day.

This means:

- Wake up every day and feel excited.

- Be the source of inspiration.

- Connect and communicate with everyone that touches the business.

- We work in a BS free zone. No politics. Zero bitching. Drama, gossip and moaning have no place here.

Putting it all together.

Nailing your *why* is one of the most important things you'll do in your business life. Until you do that, all the other advice I've given you in this book is just window dressing. Unless you act from the heart and with your heart, you won't get anywhere.

You have to believe in what you're doing and *why* you're doing it, because sincerity is impossible to fake. People will know when you genuinely believe in your *why* and they will respond positively.

If you start with your *why* and build your business using the steps I've provided for you in this book, your life will change, and you'll change the lives of others. If your *why* includes being a force for good and making the kind of impacts I've described here, I honestly believe you'll enjoy spectacular success.

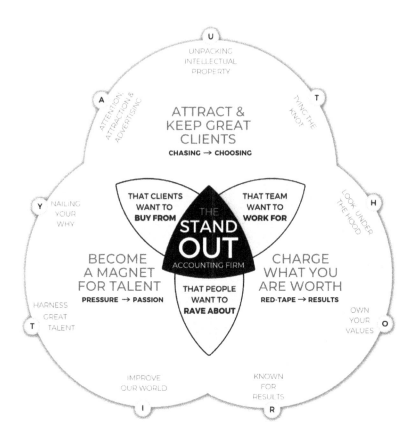

CHAPTER 11
A billion days of life changing help for families in need

Large, bold and highly impactful events, promises and phenomena really do stand out. Standing out means being extraordinary to the point where other people, initiatives and yes, accounting firms kind of recede into the background to varying degrees. But, and this is important, this book has not been a guide to pushing other hardworking businesses out of the limelight. No, this is about stepping up, and into, the spotlight and indeed shining a light on those that need help... and then doing something significant, meaningful and impactful that changes their lives for the better.

Up to this point in the book we've talked about actions and numbers, large and small, and how they ultimately create positive change. Now we are going to conclude by talking about a very large number: 1,000,000,000. One billion is a large number that can and will change a lot of lives. By giving one billion days of help in terms of water, health, food, hope to families in need, my firm belief is that we can help end extreme global poverty by 2030. And that is what The One Billion Mission (#1By2030) is all about.

Right now, you might be mentally crunching some numbers, testing hypotheses, extrapolating assumptions and if you are, you may come to the same conclusion that I did: it must be done, but I cannot do it alone. And you are right. In order to achieve this outstanding life changing ambition, accounting firms from around the world need to pool their efforts and endeavours, Stand Out in their respective areas of excellence and markets and commit to making the billion a reality.

So, back to Life Changing Accountants. Starting with the end in mind, I reverse engineered what I hope will become a movement that believes in the value of standing out by making an impact. I see a network of outstanding accounting firms making valuable contributions through their own programs and ways of working, to achieve impact driven outcomes. Yes, this ambition is teetering on the edge of being unrealistic but was this not once the case for almost every unlikely breakthrough, miraculous discovery or hard-fought battle?

The answer is yes. And I hope your answer will likewise be yes when offered the opportunity to be a part of this life changing global initiative. And if it is yes, believe me when I say, I am thrilled and moved.

1% can tip the scales in favour of families suffering extreme poverty

I'd like to think that practical, life changing advice lays at the heart of each of my books, with "Stand Out" being no exception. Staying with the accomplishment of the One Billion Mission, we have devised a simple way to integrate the necessary giving and support into your day-to-day. It's called the Tip 1% initiative.

The Tip 1% initiative challenges us to be one percent better everyday by tipping one percent of your **t**ime, **i**ncome or **p**rofit (T.I.P.) towards the One Billion Mission. The Stand Out principles support this so that taking the "One Percent Pledge" is not an onerous handicapping system rather, a satisfying, business-as-usual, "I barely felt a thing" contribution towards positive impacts for families that are desperately in need.

One percent is a big number for some. One billion is a huge

number for everyone, but I feel like we can't have one without the other — no matter how much we desperately want to do good.

But the first step is to put yourself and your firm in a position to succeed and contribute. And that's where I hope this book really helps you — in helping *you* to Stand Out.

All the best.

BONUS RESOURCES

STAND
OUT

BECOME THE ACCOUNTING FIRM THAT PEOPLE
WANT TO BUY FROM, WORK FOR & RAVE ABOUT

WANNA GO ON A DATE?

Thinking of Changing Accountants? Let's just take it easy and go on a few dates first to see if each other is 'the one'.

FIRST DATE

Learn about the 7 Smart Financial Decisions of a Cashed Up Business by Ben Walker & Harvee Pene with the **Cashed Up Book, Workshop & Scorecard.**

SECOND DATE

Let's take the next step by doing a **"Look Under the Hood"**. A $500 2nd Opinion on Tax, guaranteed to find $500 in tax savings or it's free.

THIRD DATE

Let's complete an "Urgent Need" project upfront to help claw back $$$'s in overpaid tax, get up to date with the ATO and / or set up NEW business structures.

THE PROPOSAL

We invite less than 50% of the Businesses we meet to become a client - or what we call 'join the Inspire Family'. To receive an invitation we need to know -

1 - Is there potential to ADD MASSIVE VALUE TO YOUR BUSINESS?
2 - Do we SHARE COMMON VALUES?
3 - How will you use your BUSINESS FOR GOOD?

IT'S ALL SORTED

Proactive Tax & Accounting that pays for itself in Tax Savings (av. 4 x ROI) & a Life Changing Accountant that you see 4 x times a year, to help you make Smart Financial Decisions. Starts at $600 / month + GST.

WEDDING

TOTAL FINANCIAL CONTROL

Proactive Financial Co-Pilot (Business) to help you Work 4 Days a Week, 40 Weeks a Year & Pull $400K+ Profit per Year. Starts at $600 / month + GST.

HONEYMOON

THE GOOD LIFE

Proactive Financial Co-Pilot (Personal) to help you Build $4M+ in 4 Pools of Wealth to Last 4 Generations. Starts at $600 / month + GST.

inspire™ | LIFE CHANGING ACCOUNTANTS

Cashed Up Scorecard

Benchmark your business against the 7 Smart Financial Decisions of a Cashed Up business.

YES NO

1 In the last 12 months, have you made a significant tax saving by planning it out in advance with your accountant?

2 Do you make tax deductible contributions to super each year?

3 Are you confident that you are paying your fair share in tax, and not a cent more?

4 Do you have a family trust or discretionary trust?

5 Do you use trusts to distribute profits to other family members who are in a lower tax bracket than you?

6 Do you have a motor vehicle log book that proves the percentage (%) of business use?

7 Does your business have a revenue of more than $500,000 per year?

8 Do you have a separate account (other than your main operating account) where you put money aside for profit, tax or GST?

9 Is your business profitable after you take a reasonable personal income from it?

10 Do you regularly donate to charity, churches or causes dear to your heart?

11 Do you consider yourself to be highly rewarded financially for your industry?

12 Do you have more than 3 full time staff working in your business?

13 Do you receive part or all of your revenue before you deliver your product or service?

14 Can you tell 3 months in advance if there will be a shortfall or excess of cash?

15 Do you have a recurring revenue product or service (retainer, subscription, repeat order)?

16 When presented with a BAS or Tax bill, do you usually pay them in full and on time?

17 If no revenue came in for 12 weeks, could you meet payroll and your lease payments?

18 Does your monthly recurring revenue exceed your monthly recurring expenses?

19 Is your current accountant proactive? I.e. you don't have to push him / her for ideas.

20 Do you run a business performance dashboard that shows your key performance indicators week to week?

21 Do you use a cloud based accounting system like Xero?

22 Do you (or your bookkeeper) keep your accounts up to date each month?

23 Do you have an up to date business budget and review it monthly?

24 Do you have a current business plan that you and your team review and discuss quarterly?

25 Do you earn more than 50% of your revenue from recurring sources e.g. monthly subscription?

26 Do you have a recent independent valuation for what your business is worth?

27 Do you have detailed systems & procedures in place for how things are done in your business?

28 Is your business easily saleable?

29 Has your accountant reviewed your business structure to ensure tax efficiency and asset protection in the last 12 months?

30 On paper are you worth very little, as most assets are owned in separate entities or other people's name

31 Do you know the differences between Companies, Trusts & Sole Traders?

32 Do you know if you should pay yourself a salary, a dividend, a distribution, a loan or something else?

33 Do you have an up to date Will / Estate plan in place?

34 Outside of work and family, do you have hobbies that you regularly participate in?

35 Do you typically work less hours than your team per week?

36 Are you on track to be able to retire in the next 3 - 5 years if you wanted to?

37 Are you actively paying down business & personal debt?

38 Do you regularly eat out at nice restaurants or go on date nights?

39 Can you take 8 - 12 weeks holiday each year without your business suffering?

40 Do you get more than 6 hours per night sleep?

CUT TAX

CAPTURE PROFIT

CONTROL CASHFLOW

CLAIM BIZ VALUE

COVER ASSETS

CREATE LIFESTYLE

We help Young Families use their Small Business to get Cashed Up | TOTAL | **/ 40**

"The quality of your life is the quality of decisions you make" | Tony Robbins

21 Business & Lifestyle Goals to achieve in the next 3 years

The 7 Smart Financial Decisions of a Cashed Up Business

Capture Profit	Control Cashflow		Grow Wealth	Create Lifestyle

FUTURE GOALS	Where are you now vs where do you want to be?	WHERE ARE YOU NOW?
Your Fair Share	TAX	Paying Too Much Tax
	HOURS WORKED / PER WEEK	
	BUSINESS REVENUE	
	BUSINESS PROFIT	
	BUSINESS VALUE	
	SIZE OF TEAM	
	BUSINESS END GAME	
	PERSONAL ASSETS - PROPERTY	
	PERSONAL ASSETS - SHARES	
	PERSONAL ASSETS - SUPER / SMSF	
	BUSINESS DEBT	
	PERSONAL DEBT	
	NET WEALTH	
	FREEDOM DAYS	
	GIVING BACK	
	PERSONAL HOBBIES	
	PERSONAL HEALTH	
	ANNUAL FAMILY HOLIDAYS (WEEKS PER YEAR)	
	DREAM HOLIDAY DESTINATION	
	DREAM HOLIDAY DESTINATION	
	DREAM HOLIDAY DESTINATION	
	FAMILY GOALS	
	FAMILY HOME / CAR	
	ANYTHING ELSE?	

WHAT HAS HELD YOU BACK FROM ACHIEVING THESE THINGS IN THE PAST?

TIME	MONEY	KNOWLEDGE
SUPPORT	MOTIVATION	CLEAR PLAN / LIST

Money is not the most important thing in the world. However at some point in time, money is going to control where you live, what you eat and where you choose to holiday. So it is important to plan a plan for how to pull more money out of your business, so that you can spend more time with your family and enjoy doing the things you love to do.

inspire | LIFE CHANGING ACCOUNTANTS

We help Young Families Use Their Small Business to get Cashed Up.

HAVE MORE LIVE MORE
GIVE MORE
TO YOURSELF. YOUR FAMILY. YOUR TEAM.
YOUR CLIENTS. YOUR COMMUNITY & THE WORLD.

inspire™

53 Tell tale signs you're a Cashed Up Business

(AND WHAT TO DO IF YOU'RE NOT YET CASHED UP!)

Join the inspirational team that's been featured in -

53 TELL TALE SIGNS YOU'RE A CASHED UP BUSINESS

(AND WHAT TO DO IF YOU'RE NOT YET CASHED UP!)

Dream Big. Make an Impact. Remember Your Roots.

The only thing standing between where you are right now and you being a Cashed Up Business is a series of Smart Financial Decisions. Here's 53 tell tale signs you are a Cashed Up business, having successfully made the 7 Smart Financial Decisions of a Cashed Up Business -

CUT TAX

- You own your business premises in your SMSF and have your own business pay you rent.
- You have a 'Tax War Chest' to comfortably pay you fair share in tax (and not a cent more!).
- You and all other members of your Self Managed Super Funds would be maxing out your super contributions, every year.
- You are using a Family Trust to distribute profits to lower income family members & entities (e.g. Bucket Companies) to reduce tax.
- You work closely with your accountant every year to implement legal tax saving strategies before the EOFY.
- You regularly give profits to your church and favourite charities.

CAPTURE PROFIT

- You have a small dynamic team who are paid super well.
- You are highly profitable.
- You are a Business for Good - making a major & regular contributions to charity.
- You are executing a Debt Recycling Strategy - knocking down non-tax deductible debt first.
- You have paid off your bad debt - car, credit card, personal loans etc.
- You have a personal assistant managing your inbox & calendar.
- You're always be taking advantage of the latest tech.
- You settle on a property deal every year.

CONTROL CASHFLOW

- You are paid upfront for all your products / services.
- Your revenue comes mainly from recurring sources (retainer, subscription, repeat order)
- You have an up to date Cashflow Forecast
- You can tell 3 months in advance if there will be a shortfall or excess of cash.
- You cycle business expenses through platinum credit cards for the points
- You'd use points earned from business expenses to take overseas family holidays and fly business class all the time

CHECK NUMBERS

- You have a 'Emergency Rainy Day Fund' - with 3 months of business & family life.
- You have a weekly 'slush fund' - that you could spend 100% of absolutely GUILT FREE
- You and your team would know how much money NEEDS to hit the bank account each week.
- You have a bookkeeper, financial planner, business advisor, proactive accountant and mentor.
- You are making smart financial decisions, everyday.
- You have a budget that you review regularly.
- You have a Financial Dashboard daily showing your business performance.

CRANK BUSINESS VALUE

- You have a business advisor keeping you accountable to your business performance targets
- You read a book a week
- You are a member of EO or similar exclusive access peer group
- You have a mentor and you are someone's mentor.
- You spend $100K+ annually on personal & professional development
- You, your team and or your business are winning awards for business excellence
- You love the game of business.
- You feel like you're be playing a game of real life monopoly.
- You know that success takes time, energy, creativity & diligence.
- You are in it for the long run.
- Your business would deliver incredible value, results and impact to its team, clients and community.
- You are fending off acquisition offers.
- You'd have a recent independent valuation of the business.

COVER ASSETS

- You're worth nothing on paper - making you less attractive to frivolous legal claims
- You have a comprehensive Will & Estate Plan, with all your loved ones taken care of.
- You have all your insurances sorted - Private Health, TPD, Life & Trauma etc
- You have a buy / sell agreement in place with your business partner.

CREATE LIFESTYLE

- You take 8 to 12 weeks of holiday a year
- You work in the office 2 or 3 days a week
- Your partner would work only because he / she wants to
- You have a housekeeper
- You are able to do school pick up / drop off most days you wanted
- You go on regular date nights
- You are in great physical shape and healthy
- You have a hobby you participate in regularly outside of family & business
- You regularly explore emotional, mental & spiritual development.

DREAM **BIG**
MAKE AN
IMPACT
REMEMBER YOUR ROOTS

LIFE CHANGING ACCOUNTANTS

inspire™

DAY FOR A DOLLAR
IMPACT STATEMENT

For every dollar of tax we proactively save a small business client, we give a days access to food, water, health and sanitation to a family in need.

NAME
BUSINESS
POSITION

WE LOVE TO MAKE AN IMPACT. WOULD YOU MIND IF
WE SHARED YOUR IMPACT WITH OUR COMMUNITY?

inspire™

LIFE CHANGING
ACCOUNTANTS

inspiring
BUSINESS
FOR GOOD
PODCAST with Harvee Pene

GOOD IS THE NEW GREAT

Listen on
Apple Podcasts

WE GIVE A DAY OF ACCESS TO FOOD, WATER, HEALTH OR SANITATION TO A FAMILY IN NEED, FOR EVERY DOLLAR IN TAX WE PROACTIVELY SAVE A SMALL BUSINESS.

(Our goal is 1 Billion by 2030)

inspire.business/DayforDollar

SHOOT FOR THE
MOON!

EVEN IF YOU MISS
YOU'LL LAND AMONG
THE STARS ...

inspire™

TODAY YOU WILL
INSPIRE
SOMEONE

LIFE CHANGING ACCOUNTANTS

inspire™

HERE'S TO THE CRAZY ONES

LIFE CHANGING ACCOUNTANTS

inspire™

LIVE
TO
GIVE

LIFE CHANGING ACCOUNTANTS

inspire™

ACCOUNTANTS FOR GOOD

inspire™

I HAD TOO MUCH TO DREAM LAST NIGHT...

inspire™

ACCOUNTANTS
CHANGE
LIVES

inspire™

MO' MONEY, TIME & HAPPINESS

inspire™

BUSINESSES WHO DO GOOD
DO BETTER

inspire™

DEATH BEFORE
TIMESHEETS

IT'S NOT THE

BIG THAT EAT THE SMALL,

IT'S THE ...

FAST!

THAT EAT THE SLOW.

inspire

YOU HAVE
THE POWER
TO CHANGE STUFF

inspire™

inspire™

21 Key Learnings from the
2 HR CASHED UP WORKSHOP

SAVE TAX, BOOST PROFITS & ACCELERATE CASHFLOW

Join the inspirational team that's been featured in -

21 Key Learnings from the 2 HR CASHED UP WORKSHOP

SAVE TAX, BOOST PROFITS & ACCELERATE CASHFLOW

Dream Big. Make an Impact. Remember Your Roots.

The dust has well and truly settled and I'm sure we are all back into the craziness that is our daily life. Thank you so much for letting us guide you through the 2 HR CASHED UP Workshop, I loved every minute.

Please find below 21 x Key Learnings from the Cashed Up Workshop.

And I'm also loving seeing some of you add me on instagram @HarveePene and sharing your experiences.

Please do keep in touch!

Harvee Pene
Author, TEDx Speaker & Co-Founder of Inspire - Life Changing Accountants

1 - Inspire before you Expire. If today was your last day, would you be happy with what you left behind?

2 - Family. Your Most Important Business. Knowing your WHY in Business can be as important as Knowing your NUMBERS. Business is Tough. "Business is a walk in the park ... JURASSIC PARK!" If you want to go the distance, make it through the hard times and get Cashed Up, your WHY is what will get you through. What is your why?

INSPIRE BEFORE YOU EXPIRE

3 - Life Changing Accountants.

We set out on a mission to become AU most Impactful Accounting Firm - proud to say as of today we've proactively saved our small business clients over $9M+ in Tax, which they use to reinvest back into growing their business and family.

4 - Day for Dollar. See image.

5 - Purpose Beyond Profits. "When a business has no purpose other than to succeed financially, everyone involved adopts the same mentality. Customers only buy for their personal financial gain, employees work only for financial rewards and investors only inject funds in the hope of a quick return.

WE GIVE A DAY OF ACCESS TO FOOD, WATER, HEALTH & SANITATION TO A FAMILY IN NEED, FOR EVERY DOLLAR IN TAX WE PROACTIVELY SAVE A SMALL BUSINESS.

This probably doesn't cause a problem if everyone is making money but if ever the tide turns for just a short time, everyone runs for the exit." Daniel Priestley

6 - The Cashed Up Scorecard. 40 x priorities to kickstart your Cashed Up journey. This is both a master to do list for you over the next 3 to 5 years, but also an idea of the types of smart financial decisions that a Life Changing Accountant can help you and your family to make.

7 - Four Types of Wealth - 1. Financial Wealth (Money). 2. Social Wealth (Family & Friends). 3. Physical Wealth (Health). 4. Time Wealth (Freedom). Beware of making Money, at the cost of your Family, Friends, Health & Time. "A business that makes nothing but money is a poor business." Henry Ford.

8 - Respect PARKINSONS LAW! An available resource will always be used up e.g. Time - 'if it's available, we'll use it', e.g. Food - 'if it's there, we'll eat it', e.g. Money - if it's there, we'll spend it'.

9 - Freedom Days = $Net Wealth / Cost of Living Per Day, measures true wealth based on the philosophy that what makes us truly rich is the time we have on this earth, not the money we have in our accounts.

10 - "Sales - Profit = Expenses", means that a small percentage of every dollar that comes in the door, first gets squirreled away into your Profit War Chest. For more advanced application of this formula, I recommend reading the book Profit First by Mike Michalowicz.

11 - Tax War Chest. Many business owners complain when they get a surprise bill from the ATO. So a Cashed Up business utilises a Tax War Chest to squirrel money away for PAYG, GST & Tax, so they can pay their ATO bills in full and on time.

4 TYPES OF WEALTH

12 - Is your Accountant a Dinosaur?

Charge by hour.	You push them.
Not proactive.	Not entrepreneurial.
Surprise bills.	$$ to ask questions.
Slow to respond.	No Tax Savings
Just do tax.	If any of this sounds
Not tech savvy.	familiar to you ...

It might be time to Change Accountants?

13 - Power of Compounding.

What's $1.00 doubled 20x Times? So we'd go from $1 to $2 to $4 to $8 to $16 to $32 to $64 etc ... and do that 20x times. And we get a massive $1,048,576.00! But what would happen if we taxed this magic of compounding at just 25%. So we'd go $1 to $2, less $0.25 = $1.75. Do that twenty times and you're left with just $72,570.64.

That's why it's impossible to get Cashed Up, if you're giving half your profits to the tax man!

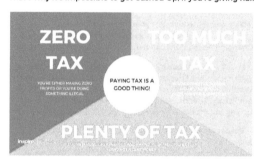

14 - Zero Tax? Too Much Tax? Plenty of Tax?

Finding ways to avoid paying tax is almost an Australian sport. And I get it, the tax man doesn't deserve a tip. But paying tax is actually a good thing! If you're paying ZERO TAX it means you're either making no profit or you're doing something illegal. If you're paying TOO MUCH TAX it means you're probably giving the tax man a tip, because your current accountant is a dinosaur. Ultimately, you want to pay PLENTY OF TAX because it means you're making great profits, and you're paying your fair share in Tax ... and not a cent more.

15 - Trusts vs Company vs Sole Trader.
On this journey called Entrepreneur-SHIP there are 3 different types of business structures or 'boats' that can help you make this journey. The correct use of business structures has been responsible for our almost $10M+ in proactive tax savings for our small business clients.

16 - The Million Dollar Pharmacist.
Remember the Pharmacist who ran 2x multimillion dollar pharmacies AND owned the buildings in which they operated. And we was a Sole Trader! Giving half his profits to the tax man. Having almost ZERO ability to legally reduce his tax. And having ALL his hard earned assets on the line. The wasn't a warning lesson about business structures, but rather about dinosaur accountants.

17 - A Family Trust is like a Jug.
We love Discretionary Trusts, because they give us the 'discretion' about who pays the tax & when. The idea: distribute the profits to family members & entities who pay tax at a lower rate than if you were a sole trader paying tax at about 50%.

18 - Never, ever, ever operate as a Sole Trader.

19 - Advanced SMSF Strategy No. 1 - Saving $96,000 a year by buying our Commercial Premises (Inspire HQ) in our Family SMSF.

We used to have a commercial lease of $12,500 + GST per month, until we bought and renovated a 200 sqm office in Fortitude Valley (1 km from Brisbane CBD) using our SMSF. My company Inspire CA now rents our office from our Family SMSF, at a 10% return for the SMSF, saving $96,000 a year for my company and 100% of the strategy is building my family wealth.

20 - Advanced SMSF Strategy No. 2 - Paying $0 Tax on $4M+ Profit. I used to not like Super because as a 30 year old it felt like it was 'forever' until I could access it. But then I learned about Parkinsons Law and realised that for me a SMSF is actually a beautiful "Retirement War Chest" - separate account, separate bank & difficult to access. For example, did you know there are 2 tax rates in Super? 15% while it's 'growing' aka in accumulation phase. 0% while it is 'going' aka in pension phase. So let's say we sell the Inspire office (owned by the SMSF) in 30 years time, and it's worth $5M. That means I can earn a $4M Profit and pay $0 Tax, legally. Imagine paying tax on $4M+ in your own name!

Inspire Office - Before

Inspire Office - During

Inspire Office - After

21 - There's 6 different ways you can pay yourself, but only 1 right way for you and your business.

In a Company you can pay yourself a Salary, a Loan (Division 7a) or a Dividend. In a Trust you can you yourself a Salary, a Loan (Drawings) or Distributions. Make sure you're pulling money out of your business the right way or risk paying thousands in excess tax.

10 DISTRIBUTION TARGETS

TARGET	WATCH FOR
1. You	$90k limit
2. Your spouse	Other income, HECS
3. Your retired parents	Self-Funded & Other Income
4. Your children	Max $416 if under 18, HECS if over
5. Your siblings	Other income, HECS, Family Tax Benefits
6. Grandparents	Self-funded & Other income
7. Superannuation	Contribution Caps
8. Church / Charity	Income tax exemption
9. Loss making business	Family Trust Election
10. Bucket company	All other income

COMPANY
- SALARY (PAYGW & SUPER)
- LOAN (DIV 7A)
- DIVIDEND

TRUST
- SALARY (PAYG & SUPER)
- LOAN (DRAWINGS)
- DISTRIBUTIONS

6 WAYS TO PULL MONEY OUT OF YOUR BUSINESS

inspire™ | LIFE CHANGING ACCOUNTANTS

inspire™ | LIFE CHANGING ACCOUNTANTS

PAY YOUR FAIR SHARE OF TAX
& NOT A CENT MORE!

$500 2ND OPINION ON TAX, GUARANTEED TO FIND $500 IN TAX SAVINGS OR IT'S FREE.

We help Young Families get Cashed Up, so they can use their **Business for Good**.

GOT A FEELING YOU'RE PAYING TOO MUCH TAX OR THAT IT'S TIME TO CHANGE ACCOUNTANTS & FINALLY GET CASHED UP?

Look Under the Hood: $500 2nd Opinion on Tax, guaranteed to find $500 in Tax Savings or it's free. We usually find $600 to $60,000 in Tax Savings, which we call your MAGIC NUMBER, so you really have nothing to lose!

Bonus for Prompt Action: The first to submit this form will receive 2 x tickets for YOU + A GUEST to the 8 HR Profit Acceleration Workshop "Get Profit" covering the 5 P's of Profit - Psychology, Priority, Predictability, Protection & Purpose, valued at $500 each.

Next Steps to get the ball rolling: Submit this form, and then *all we need are Your Most Recent Tax Returns & Financial Statements that your accountant has prepared for your family & business.* We'll get back to you in 48 hours with a 'magic number' of tax savings other opportunities we've found for you to Save Tax, Boost Profits & Accelerate Cashflow.

And for every dollar in Tax Savings that we find you, on your behalf, we'll give that many days of access to Food, Water, Health our Sanitation to a family in need. $5,000 Tax Savings = $5,000 Days of Life Changing Help to End Global Poverty.

PAYMENT TYPE (tick one)   Visa ☐   Mastercard ☐   AMEX ☐

☐ $500+GST (GUARANTEED $500 IN TAX SAVINGS OR THIS WILL BE REFUNDED TO YOU)

Your Name   . . . .

Name on Card   . . . .

Card No. ☐☐☐☐ ☐☐☐☐ ☐☐☐☐ ☐☐☐☐

Security Code ☐☐☐☐   Expiry Date . . . . . . / . . . .

(Please take a photo of this form, your tax receipt will be sent within hours)   *Prices ex. GST

WANNA GO ON A DATE?

Thinking of Changing Accountants? Let's just take it easy and go on a few dates first to see if each other is 'the one'.

FIRST DATE

Learn about the 7 Smart Financial Decisions of a Cashed Up Business by Ben Walker & Harvee Pene with the **Cashed Up Book, Workshop & Scorecard.**

SECOND DATE

Let's take the next step by doing a **"Look Under the Hood"**. A $500 2nd Opinion on Tax, guaranteed to find $500 in tax savings or it's free.

THIRD DATE

Let's complete an "Urgent Need" project upfront to help claw back $$$'s in overpaid tax, get up to date with the ATO and / or set up NEW business structures.

THE PROPOSAL

We invite less than 50% of the Businesses we meet to become a client - or what we call 'join the Inspire Family'. To receive an invitation we need to know -

1 - Is there potential to ADD MASSIVE VALUE TO YOUR BUSINESS?
2 - Do we SHARE COMMON VALUES?
3 - How will you use your BUSINESS FOR GOOD?

IT'S ALL SORTED

Proactive Tax & Accounting that pays for itself in Tax Savings (av. 4 x ROI) & a Life Changing Accountant that you see 4 x times a year, to help you make Smart Financial Decisions. Starts at $600 / month + GST.

TOTAL FINANCIAL CONTROL

Proactive Financial Co-Pilot (Business) to help you Work 4 Days a Week, 40 Weeks a Year & Pull $400K+ Profit per Year. Starts at $600 / month + GST.

THE GOOD LIFE

Proactive Financial Co-Pilot (Personal) to help you Build $4M+ in 4 Pools of Wealth to Last 4 Generations. Starts at $600 / month + GST.

inspire.business   1300 852 747   hello@inspireca.com

DREAM BIG
MAKE AN IMPACT
REMEMBER YOUR ROOTS

LIFE CHANGING ACCOUNTANTS

inspire

inspire™

LEGACY
LEGACY
LEGACY
LEGACY

inspire™

HAVE MORE

^{inspire} SO THAT YOU CAN ^{inspire}

LIVE MORE

& GIVE

MORE

INCOME
FOLLOWS
IMPACT

~~LEAVE~~ LIVE YOUR LEGACY

inspire™

DREAM BIG
THINK BIG
PLAY BIG
LIVE BIG
GIVE BIG !

inspire

PURPOSE BEYOND PROFIT

inspire

inspire

DO
GOOD
INSPIRE
OTHERS

Family.
Your most
important
business.

inspire

GOOD
IS THE NEW
GREAT

inspire

MO' MONEY, TIME & HAPPINESS

inspire™

GOAL DIGGER

INSPIRE

BEFORE YOU

EXPIRE

inspire ™

Life Changing Accountants

inspire™

Cashed Up Collateral Kit

7 KEY ASSESTS BEHIND A 7 FIGURE BUSINESS

Join the inspirational team that's been featured in -

YOU WEREN'T PUT ON THIS EARTH TO SIMPLY... BREAK EVEN

Dream Big. Make an Impact. Remember Your Roots.

In a world where INCOME FOLLOWS ASSETS, I'm here to give you all a gift from inspire. Here is an exclusive "Look Under the Hood" of the Inspire Marketing Machine and the assets we use to create a multi-million dollar revenues in our business.

1. Cashed Up Book

Supplier Contact
Minuteman Press Prahran
minuteman.press.prahran.com.au
(03) 9510 4700
viv@minuteman-prahran.com

Specifications

Cover	Text
• Print Full Colour 1 side	• 241ppPrint Black throughout
• Silk 300gsm White	• Laser 80gsm
• 0155	**Perfect Bind**
• Gloss Laminate 1 side	• Finished size 210 x 148.5mm

Download FREE copy of the book here
QTY Ordered: 1000
TOTAL Cost: $4673.35 inc GST
Average cost per book: $4.67

2. Wildly Profitable Tickets

Supplier Contact
Minuteman Press Prahran
prahran.minutemanpress.com.au
(03) 9510 4700
viv@minuteman-prahran.com

Specifications
• Printed colour 2 sides
• 400gsm artboard
• Matt laminate 2 sides
• 3D UV 1 side
• Finished size 210mm x 99mm

Download here
QTY Ordered: 1000
TOTAL Cost: $767.80 inc GST
Average cost per book: 0.80c

3. Assorted Philosophy Stickers

Supplier Contact
Oz Printing

02 8006 5177
info@ozstickerprinting.com

Specifications
- Size: 50x50mm
- Supplied: Individual (kiss cut)
- Standard Vinyl Stickers

Download

QTY Ordered: 17 designs, 1,000 pcs per design
Total QTY: 17,00
TOTAL Cost: $1683.00
Average cost per book: 0.10c

4. Cashed Up Strategy Map

Supplier Contact
Office Works Online

Specifications
- Premium Flyers
- Double Sided
- 115gsm gloss paper
- A3 (297mm x 420mm)

Download

Total QTY: 1000
TOTAL Cost: $562.00
Average cost per book: 0.56c

5. Look Under the Hood (Gift Card)

Supplier Contact
Frontline Print

02 94383000
work@front.com.au

Download

QTY Ordered: 200
TOTAL Cost: $$434.50 Inc GST
Average cost per book: $2.17

6. Sales Process: Wanna Go On a Date?

Specifications
- Print in-house
- One page brochure that outlines our Sales
- Lighten the mood and the process using the analogy of going on a Date to Getting Married.
- Double Sided
- 120gsm A4 gloss paper

Download

7. Scorecard - Cashed Up Scorecard

Specifications
- Print in-house
- Benchmark a business against the 7 Smart Financial
- One page summary of the book
- Call to action on the back to encourage further engagement
- Double Sided
- 120gsm A4 gloss paper

Take the online quiz

Download

So there you have it, THE 7 KEY ASSETS BEHIND A 7 FIGURE BUSINESS. Use these 7 assets in conjunction with a well executed campaign to quickly become a 7 figure business. Not so you can drive Ferrari's and fly private jets, but I want you to have more, so that you can live more and GIVE MORE.

Life Changing Accountants

We are numbers people and we believe that family is number one

OUR MISSION IS TO BECOME

AUSTRALIA'S MOST
IMPACTFUL
ACCOUNTING FIRM

BY GIVING THE PROACTIVE ADVICE THAT CREATES 10,000,000 FREEDOM DAYS

Introducing
HARVEE PENE
Author, TEDX Speaker & Co-Founder of Inspire

- Started first business at 14
- Bought first property at 17
- Spoke at TEDx on Achieving Big Goals
- Author of Cashed Up
- Consulted to 600+ Businesses
- Ambassador for Movember, Thankyou & B1G1 - Business for Good
- Cancer Survivor
- Young Dad

thankyou.   inspire™

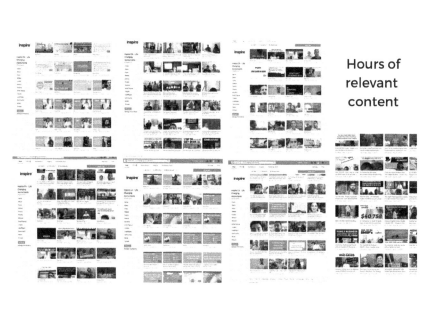

Hours of
relevant
content

Daniel Flynn shared Inspire CA - Life Changing Accountants's video
March 22, 2017

Harvee Pene and Ben love your passion to keep making an impact in our world.

Give 1,000,000 Days Campaign
02:40

7167 Views

Inspire CA - Life Changing Accountants
March 22, 2017

Introducing.... The Inspire 'Give 1,000,000 Days' Campaign!

#GIVE1MDAYS is a bold and ambitious giving goal for Inspire to give one million days worth of life-ch...

See More

Love   Comment   Share

14

View 1 more comment

Ben Walker Cheers Daniel - we're inspired to change stuff!

Give 1,000,000 Days Campaign

Inspire CA - Life Changing Accountants
about 11 months ago

Introducing.... The Inspire 'Give 1,000,000 Days' Campaign!

#GIVE1MDAYS is a bold and ambitious giving goal for Inspire to give one million days worth of life-changing water to families in need - and we're thrilled to announce it on #milliondaysofday.

https://inspireca.com/GIVE1MDAYS/

We believe that every business has the power to change lives, by integrating giving into its everyday business activities. So inspired by our friends at Thankyou, and thanks to our partnership with global giving initiative Buy One Give One (for B1G1), every time you do business with Inspire we will make a contribution to the #GIVE1MDAYS goal, and forever change the lives of families in need in the developing lands.

To follow the journey to Malawi every week and find out more about the 7 inspirational ways that doing business with us will contribute to the goal, check out the link below.

https://inspireca.com/GIVE1MDAYS/
See Less

58   44 Shares 37K Views

Like   Comment   Share

Comments   Up Next

Are You Inspires Next Accountant?
Inspire CA - Life Changing Accoun...

We help Young Families use their Small Business to get **Cashed Up**

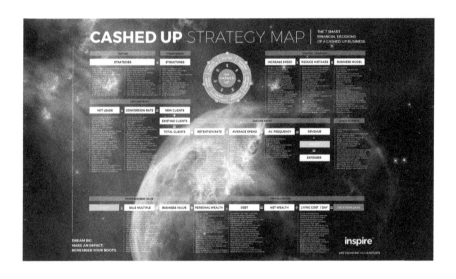

It's all
Sorted

inspire *"Top 100 Companies in Australia"*

Proactive tax and accounting service for small business that pays for itself in tax savings

Perfect for founders of 6 & 7 figure businesses, **who are in business for a purpose higher than profit.**

From $500 / month

Tax Savings / client / year = $18,000 av

3 x ROI

Dent | inspire

SYDNEY | MELBOURNE | BRISBANE

GET PROFIT

with Ben Walker & Hayden Peter
the founders of Inspire - Life-Changing Accountants
DVD + MP... | Hosted by- Glen Carlson
SME | Hosted by- Mike Reid

SAVE TAX | BOOST PROFITS | ACCELERATE CASHFLOW

FEATURED IN nab The Courier Mail xero Commonwealth Bank

CASHED UP

FREE COPY OF CASHED UP

TICKET INFO →

YOU WEREN'T PUT ON THIS EARTH TO SIMPLY BREAK EVEN

TO START MAKING MORE PROFIT AND LESS LOSS YOU WILL NEED TO

BUILD A PROFIT WAR CHEST

KNOW YOUR NUMBERS

STOP GIVING HALF YOUR PROFITS TO THE TAX MAN

inspire™

LIFE CHANGING ACCOUNTANTS

4M DAYS

OF ACCESS TO LIFE CHANGING HELP TO FAMILIES IN NEED ACROSS 16 COUNTRIES.

HELPING END GLOBAL POVERTY · FOR GOOD

We help Young Families use their Small Business to get **Cashed Up**

inspire.com

CASHED UP STRATEGY MAP

The Thinnest Document of a Cashed Up Business.

The CASHED UP Strategy Map contains over 136 different strategies to help families pull more money, time and happiness from their business – based on the best selling book CASHED UP by Ben Walker and Haines Parra.

The Strategy Map pinpoints projects for you to employ to save tax, boost profit and stabilise cashflow.

Each section shows formulas and methods for you to achieve your desired goals and having it on your wall will provide you with business improvement ideas at a glance.

Implementing just a few of those strategies every month will radically transform your business and family means effectively for many many years.

inspire™ "Top 100 Companies in Australia"

CASHED UP MASTERCLASS

A PRACTICAL 2-DAY STRATEGIC BUSINESS & LIFESTYLE PLANNING WORKSHOP

THE GOAL

Over two days you will develop a series of 12 month plans, strategies and budgets to help you pull more money, time and happiness from your business. These will become valuable assets that you will refer to on a daily or weekly basis to allow you to Boost Profits and Accelerate Cashflow in your business.

THE PROBLEM

Money is not the most important thing in the world (family is). However at some point in time, money is going to control where you live, what you eat and where you choose to holiday. So it is important to have a plan. It's incredibly difficult to build a business that gives you the freedom to put family first, without making the 7 Smart Financial Decisions of a Cashed Up Business.

CASHED UP BUSINESSES ARE ABLE TO:

- Take their family on 8 - 12 weeks a year holiday,
- Give generously to charities & causes.
- Pay themselves a decent salary.
- Build a high performing team,
- Regularly re-invest their business profits into assets like property.
- Pay down accumulated debts.
- Build a highly valuable business.
- Have the freedom to put family first.

WHAT ELSE IS COVERED?

- Create your team's individual KPI's
- Map out your Ideal Week
- Develop quarterly 'Themes' as rhythms for high level performance
- Know how much sales you need each week to reach profit targets
- Forecast when you'll be free of debt
- Plan a year's worth of family holidays
- Create plans to share with your team
- Know when to hire your next employee

WHO IS THIS WORKSHOP FOR?

Success or failure in business simply comes down to the quality of the decisions that you make. The tools we'll share in this masterclass will help business owners make smarter financial decisions, pulling more time, money and happiness from their business.

FEATURED IN -

Proactive Tax & Accounting service that pays for itself in tax savings based on implementation of "CUT TAX" in the Cashed Up method

WHAT WE'LL DO FOR YOU

- Set up Tax War Chest
- Annual Financial Statements & Tax Returns
- Proactive Tax Planning prior to 30 June
- Annual Tax saving strategies action plan
- Business Activity Statements or "BAS"
- ASIC Company Annual Review Service
- Negotiate with the ATO on your behalf
- Annual General Meeting or "AGM"
- Introductions to partners e.g. fin planners
- 3 Year Tax Forecast
- Annual Reccomendations to get Cashed Up
- Annual Business & Personal Needs Review
- Revenue, Profit & Tax report card
- Quick emails and telephone calls are FREE
- Help Desk - 24 hour guaranteed response time
- Dedicated Family Accountant
- Collaboration with Inspire Family

Year	Quarter	Theme	Month	Inspire Lifelines	ATO Deadlines
2017	Q1	Planning for Profit	Jan	CLIENT ONLY WEBINAR	
			Feb	BAS Ready by 15th February	BAS : 25th Feb
			Mar	Suprise	
	Q2	Tax Planning	Apr	Tax Planning Starts	FBT : 16th May
			May	BAS Ready by 15th May	BAS : 25th May
			Jun	CLIENT ONLY WEBINAR	107Y & Super paid : 30th June
	Q3	Tax Returns	Jul	The Handover	
			Aug	BAS Ready by 15th August	BAS : 25th August
			Sep	CLIENT ONLY WEBINAR	
	Q4	Business Performance Review	Oct	Annual General Meeting or "AGM"	
			Nov	BAS Ready by 15th November	BAS : 25th November
			Dec	CLIENT ONLY WEBINAR	
2018	Q1	Planning for Profit	Jan	CLIENT ONLY WEBINAR	
			Feb	BAS Ready by 15th February	BAS : 25th February
			Mar	"Save Tax" Book Launch	
	Q2	Tax Planning	Apr	Tax Planning Starts	FBT : 16th May
			May	BAS Ready by 15th May	BAS : 25th May
			Jun	CLIENT ONLY WEBINAR	107Y & Super paid : 30th June
	Q3	Tax Returns	Jul	The Handover	
			Aug	BAS Ready by 15th August	BAS : 25th August
			Sep	Surprise	
	Q4	Business Performance Review	Oct	Annual General Meeting or "AGM"	
			Nov	BAS Ready by 15th November	BAS : 25th November
			Dec	CLIENT ONLY WEBINAR	

ONBOARDING

	SURPRISE
Step 1	Welcome to the Inspire Family
	Thanks for changing accountants
	**Handover	Previous Accountant**
Step 2	Welcome to the Inspire Family
	Thanks for changing accountants
	Join INSPIRE FAMILY (PRIVATE)
Step 3	Welcome to the Inspire Family
	Thanks for changing accountants
	Inspire Activation Session
Step 4	Get the most out of Inspire
	Meet your dedicated accountant
	Get to know your biz & family
Step 5	What do you do
	What are your goals
	Your Business Structure Diagram
Step 6	Know how to pull money out of your biz
	Separate biz risk from personal assets
	Let us deal with ASIC for you
Step 7	We'll lodge ASIC Form 362
	free changes to address & directors
	Handover the keys to XERO
Step 8	We get real time access to your #'s
	Teach you how to do the basics

GLAD TO HAVE YOU LOOKING AFTER OUR ACCOUNTS

The Big Picture | Getting Cashed Up with Inspire

Look Under The Hood	Solve an Urgent Need	Cut Tax	Capture Profit | Control Cashflow | Check Numbers | Grow Business Value | Cover Assets		Get Cashed Up	My Family Prosperity
Second opinion on tax	Initial "Quick Win" Project	Proactive Tax & Accounting	Time saving Bookkeeping	Business coaching & advice		Wealth coaching & advice
2 Hours	First Month	Year 1 and beyond	Year 1	Year 2		Year 3
$500	POA	From $500 / m	From $300 / m	From $600 / m		From $600 / m
$500 tax savings or its free	Get the ATO off your back	$18k av. annual Tax Saving	Free up 20 hours	Double Profit & Days Off		Live the Goodlife

PULL MORE MONEY TIME AND HAPPINESS FROM YOUR BUSINESS

1YR --> 3YRS

IF YOU'RE LOOKING FOR WAYS TO SAVE TAX, BOOST PROFITS & ACCELERATE CASHFLOW, YOU NEED TO LISTEN TO BEN & HARVEE

THE DRVING FORCE BEHIND INSPIRE IS TO ENSURE ALL OF THEIR CLIENTS SUCCEED IN BUSINESS AND FAMILY LIFE.

DETAILED AGENDA WILDLY PROFITABLE!

THE HUGELY POPULAR 8 HR PROFIT ACCELERATION WORKSHOP FOR CONSCIOUS BUSINESS OWNERS TO MASTER **THE 5 P'S OF PROFIT**

Introduction | 7 steps to pull more Money, Time & Happiness from your Business, 10 am.

Priority | The 4 Bucket Cashflow Management Strategy that guarantees you'll get Cashed Up, 10:30 am.

Psychology | 6 Vital Lessons to Master the Psychology of Profit, 12 noon.

Predictability | The Ultimate Profit Formula - 10 Financial Levers You Can Pull to 10x your Revenue, Profit & Wealth, 1 pm

Protections | How to Structure Your Business to LEGALLY Reduce Tax & Cover Your ASS-ets, 3 pm

Purpose | GOOD IS THE NEW GREAT - Undeniable proof that Businesses who Do Good, Do Better, 4 pm

Conclusion | Cashed Up Hotseat with Harvee Pene Q & A on how to hit the Cashed Up Benchmark, til 5 pm

8 Agreements
of the INSPIRE FAMILY

Dream Big. Make an Impact. Remember Your Roots.

This is our version of "Terms and Conditions." Unlike a traditional T&C document, we wanted to be more human about things.

The following 8 Agreements point to the fact that in business (and in life), all we can do is manage our agreements.

We promise to be PROACTIVE, if you promise to be REACTIVE

We promise to *proactively* reach out to you every month with an idea or strategy on how you can Save Tax, Boost Profits and / or Accelerate Cashflow. That's our responsibility to you as your trusted advisor. This proactivity is why we've been able to save our clients on average $18,000+ in tax savings - or 3 x their investment in our Tax & Accounting Service. But to pull off this magic, we need you to work with us.

- Please respond to us when we need you (24 - 48 hours would be great).
- Please give us access to the information we need (we can't start a job until we have everything).
- Please take personal responsibility if we miss a deadline with the ATO, because you couldn't get things to us in time.

We like to maintain our 100% early lodgement service with the ATO and if slow responses or lack of information holds us up, we both get in their bad books.

Early lodgement means you know well in advance how to cashflow what is owed to the ATO or get your refund earlier.

Year	Quarter	Theme	Month	Inspire Lifelines	ATO Deadlines
2017	Q1	Planning for Profit	January	CLIENT ONLY WEBINAR	
			February	BAS Ready by 15th February	BAS | 28th Feb
			March	Suprise	
	Q2	Tax Planning	April	CLIENT ONLY WEBINAR	ITR's | 15th May
			May	BAS Ready by 15th May	BAS | 28th May
			June	Tax Planning	EOFY | 30th June
	Q3	Tax Returns	July	The Handover	
			August	BAS Ready by 15th August	
			September	CLIENT ONLY WEBINAR	
	Q4	Business Performance Review	October	Annual General Meeting or "AGM"	
			November	BAS Ready by 15th November	BAS | 25th November
			December	CLIENT ONLY WEBINAR	
2018	Q1	Planning for Profit	January	CLIENT ONLY WEBINAR	
			February	BAS Ready by 15th February	BAS | 28th February
			March	Suprise	
	Q2	Tax Planning	April	CLIENT ONLY WEBINAR	ITR's | 15th May
			May	BAS Ready by 15th May	BAS | 28th May
			June	Tax Planning	EOFY | 30th June
	Q3	Tax Returns	July	The Handover	
			August	BAS Ready by 15th August	BAS | 25th August
			September	CLIENT ONLY WEBINAR	
	Q4	Business Performance Review	October	Annual General Meeting or "AGM"	
			November	BAS Ready by 15th November	BAS | 25th November
			December	CLIENT ONLY WEBINAR	

See Annual Calendar of Activities

Stop doing the books, and start doing better business

We reckon there's better things you could be doing with your time than doing your bookkeeping. The average business owner spends 10 - 20 hours per month doing bookkeeping, which we believe could be better reinvested back into your business and your life. So maybe not year one, but definitely from year two onwards we want you to give up the bookkeeping and either engage Inspire to do it or another quality bookkeeper - either way your DIY bookkeeping days are numbered...

Become a Business for Good

We believe that business should be the driving force behind creating a better world. That's why as we help you get Cashed Up - by making smarter financial decisions - we will encourage you to find ways to give back and become what we call a "Business for Good". One that gives part of its profits to making the world a better place. We've partnered with global giving initiative B1G1 Business for Good to make business giving easy, and hope you will too.

Talk about us behind our back

Some of our best clients have come from referrals - aka when we do a good job and clients talk about us behind our backs. For the first time in our lives, this is actually a good thing. We would hope that after we've delivered some great value to you (Save Tax, Boost Profits, Accelerate Cashflow) that you will give consideration to referring us to at least 2 other business people who you believe would benefit from the work we do.

We love you, but we won't go to jail for you

If you want us to do anything illegal, shady or unethical, we're definitely NOT the right accountant for you. That involves not declaring cash, claiming deductions that aren't allowed or crossing the line of the law. We'll help you execute every legally available strategy to help you save tax, but we're not in the game of doing anything illegal. You cool with that?

Please pay your bills on time

If we're delivering what we promised and you aren't paying your bills on time, well then the laws of exchange are out of balance. And that's not fair on everyone else who is paying on time. Or our Team, who are working hard for you. So if your account is more than 30 days in arrears, we'll attempt to charge your card without further notice, per our original Agreement. If payments continue to be unsuccessful, we'll have to limit your access to our service until you are up to date.

Be a good human.

There is no room for rude, insulting or general bad behaviour and anyone being anything other than a cool human will be asked to leave the Inspire Family. This goes for clients (you) as well as our Inspire Team and Business Partners.

You get what you pay for.

When you join the "It's all sorted" tax and accounting service, you get –

WHAT WE'LL DO FOR YOU
Set up Tax War Chest
Annual Financial Statements & Tax Returns
Proactive Tax Planning prior to 30 June
Annual Tax saving strategies action plan
Business Activity Statements or "BAS"
ASIC Company Annual Review Service
Negotiate with the ATO on your behalf
Annual General Meeting or "AGM"
Introductions to partners e.g. fin planners
3 Year Tax Forecast
Annual Reccomendations to get Cashed Up
Annual Business & Personal Needs Review
Revenue, Profit & Tax report card
Quick emails and telephone calls are FREE
Help Desk - 24 hour guaranteed response time
Dedicated Family Accountant
Collaboration with Inspire Family

We'll more than happily have quick phone call or answer an email (within 24 hours) but if something falls out of scope, we'll do the right thing and give you an upfront price for that project.

Some examples of projects or advice that fall outside the scope of tax & accounting -

- Bookkeeping
- Advice on CGT of an asset - selling a property or business
- Setting up a new structure
- Preparing business performance reports such as P & L, Balance Sheet or a Business Budget.
- Preparing financial reports for your board meeting or award application.

My promise to you

I promise to return your phone call or email within 24 hours - outside of weekends and public holidays.

I promise to treat you like I would my family. That means that I won't recommend anything to you that I wouldn't recommend to my mother or sister. It also means that if I don't think what you're doing is a good idea I'll let you know.

I promise to be your trusted advisor. This means I'll keep everything we say and everything I know about your family and your business in confidence. It also means I'll do everything in my power to help you make smarter financial decisions.

It's all
Sorted

inspire™ *"Top 100 Companies in Australia"*

Proactive tax and accounting service for small
business that pays for itself in tax savings

WE ARE NUMBERS PEOPLE

AND WE BELIEVE **FAMILY IS NUMBER ONE**

Our Family First Philosophy

"The most precious thing in life we have are moments. Let's make the most of them before they disappear.

See the world while we still can. And cherish those while they're still here. When our lives are almost over, it won't matter how much money we made, or hours we worked or number of times we got employee of the month.

When we look back it will be all about the memories we made, the hours we spent with those we love and where we father of the month, mother of the year or friend of the lifetime."

Prince Ea

The Problem | Business owners are paying way too much tax. Why?

Your accountant isn't proactive

Everyone pays tax. But hidden within the tax you pay, is tax you don't need to pay. The only way to tell the difference between the two, is through proactive advice from your accountant.

Your accountant charges by the hour

Many old school accountants get too focused on clocking time, and not enough time on making an impact - like saving you tax. The Founders of Inspire CA both promised to never charge a client using timesheets, after seeing many dishonest practices in the industry.

Your accountant is slow to respond

If you're a small fish - in the eyes of your accountant - it can take days, weeks or even months to get a response. And when they do respond, you fear getting slapped with a bill. This lack of communication can almost guarantee that you are not taking advantage of cutting edge tax strategy.

10 Signs Your Accountant is a Dinosaur

- Charge by hour
- Not proactive
- Surprise bills
- Slow to respond
- Just do tax
- Not tech savvy
- You push them
- Not entrepreneurial
- $$ to ask questions
- No Tax Savings

TIME TO CHANGE ACCOUNTANTS?

I'VE NEVER SEEN SUCH GROOVY, AMAZING AND CONNECTED ACCOUNTANTS IN MY LIFE.

PHILLIP DI BELLA | DI BELLA COFFEE

Does your accountant make you money or take your money?

We are well known for a campaign we ran two years ago called Save $500,000 Tax. It was a bold and audacious target to save our clients half million dollars in tax by proactively implementing cutting edge tax saving strategies.

We didn't think we'd actually get the $500,000 tax savings but we knew that we had to **GO BIG or GO HOME**.

We ended up saving our clients a huge $1.26M in tax in 12 short weeks and went on to be name Top 100 Companies in Australia and featured on many platforms including The DENT Podcast, Small Business Big Marketing, The Courier Mail and TEDx, to name a few.

Most importantly since that "Save Tax" campaign we've now been able to help our clients save a total $2.6M dollars in tax by implementing cutting edge tax saving strategies.

That's about $18,000 in tax savings for each business we serve, which means our tax & accounting service pays for itself 3 - 4 times. Our clients tell us they use these savings to reinvest back into growing their businesses and taking their families on holiday. **What would you do with $18k?**

Annual General Meeting | advice to make next year the best yet.

An AGM or Annual General Meeting is a very special service we do when your ANNUAL FINANCIAL STATEMENTS AND TAX RETURNS are done, to give you recommendations on how to make the next financial year the best year yet. Together we'll cover -

- Report Card: How much Revenue, Profit & Tax did I make / pay this year compared to last?
- Tax Forecast: How much tax can I expect to pay in the next 3 years and when?
- Tax War Chest: How much tax should I set aside in a separate bank account this year?
- Get Cashed Up: 3 recommendations to make 2018 the best year yet
- And more.

SERIOUS VALUE IN UNDERSTANDING AND
RECEIVING CLARITY AROUND OUR BUSINESS
NUMBERS AND FIGURES. I FEEL CONFIDENT!

NAT TAYLOR | CONCRETE TRAINING

Tax War Chest | No more surprise tax bills with no way to pay.

The Problem | In a world where we tend to spend what we earn, it's common to find ourselves at the end of the year with a ATO bill but no money to pay for it.
This can cause high levels of panic, stress and anger. Repeat this cycle over time and the ATO may shut your business down.

> **The Old Way |** Get paid > Pay bills > Get tax bill > Panic > Stress > Anger > Miss Payment > Get Fined > Start ATO Payment Plan > No Profit.

The Solution | Setting aside a small portion of every invoice that comes in ensures that you have enough in your reserve to pay your invoices in full and on time. It also ensures you aren't funding your business on someone else's money.

> **The Inspire Way |** Get paid > Set aside 15% in Profit War Chest > Pay bills > Get Tax Bill > Pay Tax Bill > In Full > On Time > Stress Less

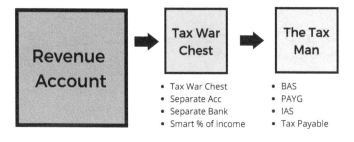

Revenue Account	→	Tax War Chest	→	The Tax Man
		• Tax War Chest		• BAS
		• Separate Acc		• PAYG
		• Separate Bank		• IAS
		• Smart % of income		• Tax Payable

I HATE PAYING TAX ... BUT HAVING A TAX WAR CHEST WITH MONEY IN IT MAKES PAYING THE BILLS SO MUCH LESS STRESSFUL

Proactive Tax Planning | Stop giving half your profits to the tax man.

No one wants to give the Tax Man a tip, right? So at Inspire we will proactively take you through a process in April to June every year called Tax Planning. This is about exploring every legally available tax saving strategy based on the current laws and looking for ways to help you implement them. On average we've saved our clients $18,000+ in tax each year, which is how our accounting services can pay for itself.

Here are some of the Tax Saving strategies and the impacts they have made on small business owners.

TAX SAVING **STRATEGY** TAX SAVING **IMPACT**

DISTRIBUTE PROFITS TO A COMPANY		THAT'S $38K I DON'T HAVE TO PAY THE GOVERNMENT	
MAX OUT YOUR SUPER CONTRIBUTIONS!		$28,207 TAX SAVED. HOLIDAY TIME!	
WRITE OFF BAD DEBTS BEFORE EOFY		$35,067 TAX SAVED. BUYING BITCOIN.	
DON'T PAY TAX ON $ NOT YET RECEIVED		$32, 811 TAX SAVED. INVEST IN PROPERTY.	
DISTRIBUTE PROFITS TO RETIRED PARENTS		$9,157 TAX SAVED. BUILDING A DECK!	
KEEP A MOTOR VEHICLE LOG BOOK		$9,757 TAX SAVED. BARCELONA HOLIDAYS!	

Make BAS work for you | Turn a BAS Deadline into a BIZ Lifeline.

Most business owners hate BAS time, but Cashed Up business owners realise that a BAS Deadline can actually be a BIZ Lifeline - if you know your numbers. That's why we aim to lodge your BAS early - so you don't get lumped with an unexpected bill with short notice. We also host a webinar to help you review your business performance based on the reports in Xero that are no up to date, thanks to the BAS deadline.

3 year tax forecast | Because nobody likes *surprise* tax bills

We like some surprises - flowers, weekend away, date night - but not Tax Surprises. If you've had a surprise tax bill before you'll know the frustration (and sometimes even anger).

So not only are we constantly implementing strategies to ensure you only pay your fair share (and not a cent more) we also maintain a 3 year tax forecast for you = no surprises.

I NO LONGER HATE
TAX & ACCOUNTANTS

INSPIRE TAKES THE FEAR
AWAY FROM NUMBERS

2018	2019	2020

Inspirational Accountants by your side

QUICK RESPONSE

We're here for you at help@inspireca.com. *We promise to get back to you in 24 hours, or we'll send you a bunch of flowers!*

HELP DESK

Quick phone calls and emails are free. We'd hate for you to make a major financial decision without running it past us first.

INSPIRE FAMILY (PRIVATE)

Network & collaborate with our family accountants and other clients of inspire in our private Facebook Group.

CLIENT ONLY WEBINARS

Join the co-founders of Inspire CA for exclusive webinars on how to get Cashed Up.

Accountants for Good

At Inspire we believe that every business has the power to change lives by integrating giving into it's everyday activities. Thanks to our partnership with global giving initiative B1G1, we see a bright future full of giving. So Thankyou, no just for being a client but for making a real difference as well.

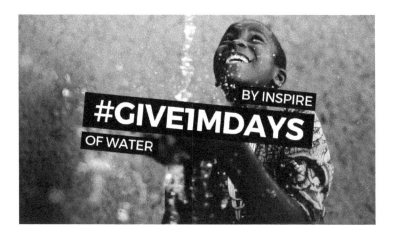

Give 1,000,000 Days is a bold and ambitious giving goal for Inspire to give one million days worth of life-changing water to families in need.

Go to inspireca.com/giving-back/ for the latest giving update.

Cashed Up | Pull more money, time and happiness from your business.

Money is NOT the most important thing in the world. However at some point in time, money is going to control where you live, what you eat and where you choose to holiday. So it's important to have a plan. A plan for how to pull more money out of your business. If you want to get Cashed Up, your plan must address these 7 steps -

Cut Tax

It's almost impossible to get Cashed Up when you're giving half your profits to the tax man. Having a proactive accountant who can help you implement deliver cutting edge tax strategies will ensure you pay the least amount of tax legally possible.

Capture Profits

In a world where we spend what we earn, protecting your profit is essential. If you don't have a profit improvement plan, regardless of how much money you earn, you will always struggle.

Control Cashflow

Simply growing your business is no longer enough, if you want to escape the cash crisis permanently. You need to get paid faster and be in control. In a time when "Cash is King", are you ruling it or is cash ruling you?

Check Numbers

Business owners who know their numbers have a tremendous advantage over those who do not. Your financials tell a story - and understanding the story behind your numbers can be one of the most important ingredients for long-term success.

Crank Business Value

Most business owners actually own a job not a business. Think about it, when you go on holiday does your cashflow go on holidays too? A Cashed Up business can be your most valuable asset. Let's start building it.

Cover Assets

Once you've begun to get Cashed Up, you become a target for financial predators. It starts with being worth nothing on paper and ends with the smart use of structures to separate business risks from personal assets - like the family home.

Create Lifestyle

It's almost impossible to get Cashed Up when you're giving half your profits to the tax man. Having a proactive accountant who can help you implement deliver cutting edge tax strategies will ensure you pay the least amount of tax legally possible.

Get
Cashed Up.

If you think it's about Tax & Accounting,
you've missed the point. it's about
pulling more money, time and
happiness out of your business.

inspire™ *"Top 100 Companies*
in Australia"

The Back Story

It's important to know the WHO, WHAT & WHY
of inspire before you Change Accountants

Best Mates & Business Partners, Ben Walker & Harvee Pene are both numbers people and believe that **FAMILY IS NUMBER ONE.**

After connecting with eachother through the Global Giving Initiative, Buy One Give One (B1G1) & realising they had a shared value of **DOING GOOD**

Together they started Inspire - Life Changing Accountants 5 years ago

OUT OF DEEP FRUSTRATION

after working in many of the Top Accounting firms around Australia.

Frustration that Accountants were largely **reactive**, slow to adopt technology, charged by the hour and only helped their clients once or twice a year.

We thought, what if instead
of reporting on history
(by just doing Tax Returns),
what if as Accountants
we could help our clients ...

MAKE HISTORY
DO GOOD
& GET CASHED UP

Co-Founders Ben Walker & Harvee Pene   inspire | LIFE CHANGING ACCOUNTANTS

Wanting to help **Young Families get Cashed Up, so they can use their Business for Good,** Ben & Harvee wrote the book and mapped out the 7 Smart Financial Decisions of a Cashed Up Business.

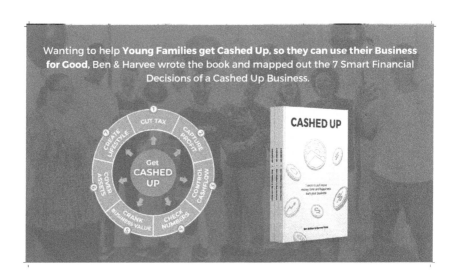

It's all Sorted

 inspire™ "Top 100 Companies in Australia"

Proactive tax and accounting service for small business that pays for itself in tax savings

And that's where **"IT'S ALL SORTED"** was born ....

PROACTIVE TAX & ACCOUNTING THAT PAYS FOR ITSELF IN TAX SAVINGS.

(AND A LIFE CHANGING ACCOUNTANT TO HELP YOU MAKE THE 7 SMART FINANCIAL DECISIONS OF A CASHED UP BUSINESS.)

In a world where most Accountants are Dinosaurs

- Charge by hour
- Not proactive
- Surprise bills
- Slow to respond
- Just do tax
- Not tech savvy
- You push them
- Not entrepreneurial
- $$ to ask questions
- No Tax Savings

"IT'S ALL SORTED" solves the top 5 problems business owners have with their current Accountant

PROBLEM #1

I hate asking my
Accountant
questions
because I either
never get a
response or I get
slapped with a bill!

PROBLEM #1

I hate asking my Accountant questions because I either never get a response or I get slapped with a bill!

IT'S ALL SORTED

PROACTIVE TAX & ACCOUNTING THAT
PAYS FOR ITSELF IN TAX SAVINGS

Quick Calls & Emails are FREE, with a guaranteed 24 hour response time.

WHY? We want to know if you've got something on your mind (e.g. Buying a Car) so we can help you make a smart financial decision.

inspire | LIFE CHANGING ACCOUNTANTS

PROBLEM #2

I hate getting
surprise bills from
my Accountant or
the ATO that hurt
my cashflow.

inspire | LIFE CHANGING
ACCOUNTANTS

PROBLEM #2

I hate getting
surprise bills from
my Accountant or
the ATO that hurt
my cashflow.

IT'S ALL SORTED

PROACTIVE TAX & ACCOUNTING THAT
PAYS FOR ITSELF IN TAX SAVINGS

**We lodge your BAS 2 weeks
early and help you maintain
a healthy "TAX WAR CHEST"**

WHY? So you can pay your bills in
full, on time and with no stress.

inspire™ | LIFE CHANGING
ACCOUNTANTS

PROBLEM #3

I only see my Accountant once a year, it's only ever reactive or about the past.

inspire | LIFE CHANGING ACCOUNTANTS

PROBLEM #3

I only see my
Accountant once
a year, it's only
ever reactive or
about the past.

IT'S ALL SORTED

PROACTIVE TAX & ACCOUNTING THAT
PAYS FOR ITSELF IN TAX SAVINGS

**We host 3 x Proactive
Future Focused Meetings
with you each Year.**

WHY? Because in January you need
to set Goals, in May you need to
save Tax and in September you
need an "AGM" to make this
financial year your best yet.

inspire | LIFE CHANGING
ACCOUNTANTS

PROBLEM #4

The Banks won't give me finance because either my income is too low (to keep my Tax down) or I'm constantly waiting on my accountant for up to date financials.

PROBLEM #4

The Banks won't give me finance because either my income is too low (to keep my Tax down) or I'm constantly waiting on my accountant for up to date financials.

IT'S ALL SORTED

PROACTIVE TAX & ACCOUNTING THAT
PAYS FOR ITSELF IN TAX SAVINGS

We prepare your Tax Returns & Financial Statements for Your Businesses, Investments & Family early in the new financial year.

WHY? As Accountants & mortgage brokers, we can work our magic to keep your income low for tax purposes but still able to access great finance options to accelerate your goals.

inspire | LIFE CHANGING ACCOUNTANTS

PROBLEM #5

No matter how much more Revenue I earn, there's still little or no Profit leftover, for all my hard work.

PROBLEM #5

No matter how much more Revenue I earn, there's still little or no Profit leftover, for all my hard work.

IT'S ALL SORTED

PROACTIVE TAX & ACCOUNTING THAT PAYS FOR ITSELF IN TAX SAVINGS

We help you maintain a healthy "PROFIT WAR CHEST"

WHY? Because when you squirrel away a healthy percentage of every dollar you earn, you have enough for a rainy day, paying off debt & reinvesting into the business.

inspire | LIFE CHANGING ACCOUNTANTS

It's all
Sorted

 inspire™ "Top 100 Companies in Australia"

Proactive tax and accounting service for small business that pays for itself in tax savings

"IT'S ALL SORTED"

On average our clients pay us about $500 + GST per month.

And on average we've delivered about $18,000 in Tax Savings each year for each client.

That's a 3 x ROI!

In fact, given we're in the business of making Smart Financial Decisions ...

We wouldn't even invite you to become a client of ours unless we were confident we could pay for ourselves in Tax Savings.

<50%

CAN WE ADD MASSIVE VALUE?

DO WE SHARE COMMON VALUES?

We help Young Families get Cashed Up, so they can use their **Business for Good**

<50%

CAN WE ADD MASSIVE VALUE?

<50%

CAN WE ADD MASSIVE VALUE?

DO WE SHARE COMMON VALUES?

<50%

CAN WE ADD MASSIVE VALUE?

DO WE SHARE COMMON VALUES?

We help Young Families get Cashed Up, so they can use their **Business for Good**

THE TOP 100 PODCAST SHOWCASING OUR BEST CLIENTS

INSPIRING BUSINESS FOR GOOD

Inspirational stories of businesses that exist for good - the good of their founders, their team, their clients and the world.

Harvee's goal is to deconstruct how business leaders make an impact and ultimately prove that **businesses who do good, do better.**

- Effective Giving and One for One.
- Business model design.
- Vision, Mission & Values led growth.
- Impact at scale.
- Revenue, Profit & Cashflow drivers.
- Attracting top talent.

- World class Leadership.
- And Leaving, Living and Leveraging a Legacy.

BUSINESS FOR GOOD

PJ Patterson on Leaving a Legacy & T
Inspiring Business for Good — 6 March

"Inspiring Business for Good is like sitting down & chatting with an amazing mentor over coffee each week. Harvee pulls out the gold from each person so that you can make the changes in your business "to inspire & do good." - **Emma Small**

thankyou. **inspire**™

Ultimately we exist to help Young Families get Cashed Up, so they can use their Business for Good.

So what GOOD do you want to do for yourself, your family, your team, your clients, your community, your industry and even the world?

(Give us a great answer to that question, and we'd love to welcome you into the "Inspire Family".)

HAVE MORE LIVE MORE
GIVE MORE

TO YOURSELF. YOUR FAMILY. YOUR TEAM.
YOUR CLIENTS. YOUR COMMUNITY & THE WORLD.

FRONT WITHOUT GIFT CARD ATTACHED

FRONT WITH GIFT CARD ATTACHED

BACK

GOT A FEELING THAT
YOU ARE PAYING TOO MUCH TAX?

Fold here to see how the print backs up

To redeem this giftcard for full terms and conditions visit:
www.inspireca.com/giftcard

You don't really think the tax man deserves a tip do you?

inspire   This gift card is not redeemable for cash

FRONT   BACK

FRONTLINE PRINT

MARK SALCEDO | PRE PRESS
P: 02 9438 3000   F: 02 9436 3206
E: art@front.com.au

PLEASE READ SPECIAL INSTRUCTIONS
1. When proof reading please CIRCLE or CROSS OUT the incorrect word / object and show correction clearly.
2. Please reply to this email or fax (02) 9436 3206 to proceed with the order.

Please note that the customer is responsible for checking all the details including spelling and once approval is given to proceed by email or fax any changes or re-printing required will be at the customers expense.

By approving via email or fax I understand and agree that the artwork proof shown here is to my satisfaction and I am authorizing Frontline Print the use of the artwork to proceed with my order. Approving this artwork I understand and agree the production turn around starts from the date of artwork approval.

I understand and agree payment must be paid in full before the order is sent out (*excluding 30 day accounts).

DATE: 12 / 03 / 18   JOB NO: 205 610
JOB NAME: INSPIRE GIFT CARDS
COMPANY: INSPIRE
CONTACT: HARVEE PENE   TOTAL QTY: 2000

SIGNATURE	DATE

PLASTIC CARDS	☑ 0.76mm ☐ 0.50mm	☐ SEQUENTIAL BARCODES	STARTING AT: .... ☐ Code 128 ☐ Code 39 ☐ EAN ☐ Interleaved 2 of 5	☐ SIGNATURE STRIPE	☐ SCRATCH PANELS
PRINTED CMYK	☑ Two Sides ☐ One Side ☐ B/W Back ☐ Blank Back	☐ SEQUENTIAL NUMBERING	STARTING AT: .... SIZE: .... FONT: .... COLOUR:	☐ PVC CARD - OVER LAMINATE FOR THERMAL PRINTING ☐ PVC CARD - MAGNETIC STRIPE ☐ HI-CO ☐ LO-CO	
CARD SIZE	☑ 85x54mm with Round Corners	☐ VARIABLE DATA (DATABASE SUPPLIED)	STARTING AT: .... SIZE: .... FONT: .... COLOUR:	☐ ENCODING ☐ Track 1 ☐ Track 2 ☐ Track 3	
CARD FINISH	☑ Gloss 2/S	☐ 4MM DRILL HOLE	☐ LANYARD SLOT HOLE	MANUFACTURE TIME (FROM APPROVAL) ☐ 1-2 Days ☐ 4-6 Days ☑ 10 Days ☐ 14 Days (PVC Cards)	

ANY OTHER OPTIONS: ....

WANNA GO ON A DATE?

Thinking of Changing Accountants? Let's just take it easy and go on a few dates first to see if each other is 'the one'.

FIRST DATE

Learn about the 7 Smart Financial Decisions of a Cashed Up Business by Ben Walker & Harvee Pene with the **Cashed Up Book, Workshop & Scorecard.**

SECOND DATE

Let's take the next step by doing a **"Look Under the Hood"**. A $500 2nd Opinion on Tax, guaranteed to find $500 in tax savings or it's free.

THIRD DATE

Let's complete an "Urgent Need" project upfront to help claw back $$$'s in overpaid tax, get up to date with the ATO and / or set up NEW business structures.

THE PROPOSAL

We invite less than 50% of the Businesses we meet to become a client - or what we call 'join the Inspire Family'. To receive an invitation we need to know -

1 - Is there potential to ADD MASSIVE VALUE TO YOUR BUSINESS?
2 - Do we SHARE COMMON VALUES?
3 - How will you use your BUSINESS FOR GOOD?

IT'S ALL SORTED

Proactive Tax & Accounting that pays for itself in Tax Savings (av. 4 x ROI) & a Life Changing Accountant that you see 4 x times a year, to help you make Smart Financial Decisions. Starts at $600 / month + GST.

TOTAL FINANCIAL CONTROL

Proactive Financial Co-Pilot (Business) to help you Work 4 Days a Week, 40 Weeks a Year & Pull $400K+ Profit per Year. Starts at $600 / month + GST.

THE GOOD LIFE

Proactive Financial Co-Pilot (Personal) to help you Build $4M+ in 4 Pools of Wealth to Last 4 Generations. Starts at $600 / month + GST.

inspire.business   1300 852 747   hello@inspireca.com

Factory 4 / 87 Reserve Road, Artarmon NSW 2064
Phone: + 61 2 9438 3000 • **Fax:** +61 2 9436 3206
Email: Accounts@front.com.au
Website: www.front.com.au

ABN 66 614 008 838 • ACN 614 008 838

DIGITAL SHEET PRINTING | WIDE FORMAT | DIGITAL ROLL LABELS | FLEXOGRAPHIC | HOT FOIL STAMPING | THERMAL | INKJET

Date:	12/02/18	Quote No: **184204**
Company:	INSPIRE	
Att:	HARVEE PENE	
From:	Jay Lanka	
Subject:	**PLASTIC LOYALTY CARDS & HANGSELL CARDHOLDERS**	

Hi Harvee

Thank you for the opportunity to quote, I have listed below the relevant prices and details;

0.76MM PLASTIC CARDS PRINTED FULL COLOUR
2 SIDES WITH GLOSS FINISH AND TRIMMED TO
85 X 54MM WITH ROUNDED CORNERS.
STD 10 WORKING DAYS T/AROUND

200 X HANGSELL CARDHOLDERS
SIZE :105MM X 150MM
PRINTED FULL COLOUR BOTH SIDES.
CELLOGLAZE BOTH SIDES. (GLOSS / MATT)
CARDS = $155 plus GST & CARDHOLDERS = $220 plus GST

Quantity :	200
PRINT	375.00
FREIGHT	20.00
SUBTOTAL($)	395.00
GST($)	39.50
TOTAL($)	434.50

Please call me if you have any further questions or would like to place an order.

Regards,

Please contact the sender on (02) 9438-3000 if there is a problem with this transmission.

inspire | LIFE CHANGING ACCOUNTANTS

YOUR PERSONAL BUSINESS PLAN

Year

Level Number	Level 1	Level 2	Level 3	Level 4	Level 5	Level 6	Level 7
Level Name	Coal	Bronze	Silver	Gold	Platinum	Platinum One	Diamond
Position Title	Jnr Accountant	Jnr Account Manager	Account Manager	Snr Account Manager	Team Leader		
Nickname	JAC	JAM	AM	SAM	TM	BM	CM
Salary Range	$30,000	$40,000	$50,000	$65,000			
Salary Range	$40,000	$55,000	$70,000	$85,000			
Profit Share?	Not Yet	Not Yet	Not Yet	Getting Close	Yes	Yes	Yes
Client #	10 (Bookkeeping)	10	20	30	40	45	50
Client $	3,000	6,000	6,000	6,000	7,500	9,000	15,000
Mastery	BAS, XERO, ITR & FS, Offshore Jobs	Sales Process	Tax Plan, Structures, ACM	Total Financial Control	The Good Life	Lead a Team	Lead multiple teams
Education	B Bus (Acc)	Start CA	CA in Progress	CA	Tax Agent	Dip FP	MBA
Book 1	Cashed up, Ben & Harvee	Entrepreneur Revolution, D Priestley	Delivering Happiness, Tony Hsieh	Traction, Gino Wickman	Rework, Jason Fried	Influence, Robert Cialdini	Barefoot Investor, Scott Pape
Book 2	Chapter One, Daniel Flynn	Profit First, Mike Michalowicz	Unprofessional, Jack Delosa	Buying Customers, Brad Sugars	The Virgin Way, Richard Branson	Good to Great, Jim Collins	Legacy, James Kerr
Book 3	The Perfect Firm, Rob Nixon	The Four Hour Work Week, Tim Ferris	Built to Sell, John Warrillow	Pumpkin Plan, Mike Michalowicz	24 Assets, Daniel Priestley	Cash Flow Quadrant, Kiyosaki	Unlimited Power, Tony Robbins

YOUR PERSONAL BUCKET LIST

Year							
FAMILY / HEALTH							
COMMUNITY / CONTRIBUTION							
CAREER / WEALTH							

DREAM BIG. MAKE AN IMPACT. REMEMBER YOUR ROOTS.

inspire | LIFE CHANGING ACCOUNTANTS

YOUR PERSONAL BUSINESS PLAN

Year

	Level 1	Level 2	Level 3	Level 4	Level 5	Level 6	Level 7
Level Number	Level 1	Level 2	Level 3	Level 4	Level 5	Level 6	Level 7
Level Name	Coal	Bronze	Silver	Gold	Platinum	Platinum One	Diamond
Position Title	Jnr Accountant	Jnr Account Manager	Account Manager	Snr Account Manager	Team Leader		
Nickname	JAC	JAM	AM	SAM	TM	BM	CM
Salary Range	$30,000	$40,000	$50,000	$65,000			
Salary Range	$40,000	$55,000	$70,000	$85,000			
Profit Share?	Not Yet	Not Yet	Not Yet	Getting Close	Yes	Yes	Yes
Client #	10 (Bookkeeping)	10	20	30	40	45	50
Client $	3,000	6,000	8,000	6,000	7,500	9,000	15,000
Mastery	MAS, XERO, ITR & FS, Offshore role	Sales Process	TaxPlan, Structures, ACM	Total Financial Control	The Good Life	Lead a Team	Lead multiple teams
Education	B Bus (Acc)	Start CA	CA in Progress	CA	Tax Agent	Dip FP	MBA
Book 1	Cashed Up, Ben & Harvee	Entrepreneur Revolution, D Priestley	Delivering Happiness, Tony Hsieh	Traction, Gino Wickman	Rework, Jason Fried	Influence, Robert Cialdini	Barefoot Investor, Scott Pape
Book 2	Chapter One, Daniel Flynn	Profit First, Mike Michalowicz	Unprofessional, Jack Delosa	Buying Customers, Brad Sugars	The Virgin Way, Richard Branson	Good to Great, Jim Collins	Legacy, James Kerr
Book 3	The Perfect Firm, Rob Nixon	The Four Hour Work Week, Tim Ferris	Built to Sell, John Warrillow	Pumpkin Plan, Mike Michalowicz	2X Assets, Daniel Priestley	Cashflow Quadrant, Kiyosaki	Unlimited Power, Tony Robbins

YOUR PERSONAL BUCKET LIST

Year

FAMILY / RELATIONSHIPS							
COMMUNITY / CONTRIBUTION							
CAREER / WEALTH							

DREAM BIG. MAKE AN IMPACT. REMEMBER YOUR ROOTS.

Thankyou

WEEKLY GRATITUDE CIRCLE

Dream Big. Make an Impact. Remember Your Roots.

Welcome to our weekly Thankyou Circle. Allow me to kick off this standing team gratitude circle by reminding us all of some key principles -

One of the most powerful words we can say is "Thankyou", because gratitude is a the great multiplier.

Be thankful for what you do have in your life, and you tend to get more of it. In reverse, complain about what you don't have in life, and you tend to get less of it.

How Team Thankyou works is we gather around in a circle and thank each other for the impact you've seen (or heard) someone make in the last week.

For example -

"Ethan I want to Thankyou for coming around and cleaning up the bins and everyone's workstations. It really made for an fresh working environment and it made my life easier. Thankyou,"

"Kathryn I want to thank you for proactively calling the ATO and negotiating the a penalties and interest remission for the Greer Family Trust. They really appreciated it and were so surprised with the 'out of the blue' refund."

Team Thankyou is the one time each week that we step aside from the busy-ness that is Inspire. and remind ourselves of the impact we've each made and how grateful we are to be surrounded by people who inspire us.

The idea is we never ever leave a Thankyou circle without feeling acknowledge and appreciated for the impact we've made.

There's no order or time limit. "So [Name] would you like to kick us off?"

We are numbers people and we believe that FAMILY IS NUMBER ONE.

POSITION DESCRIPTION

LIFE CHANGING ACCOUNTANT
Getting tax sorted, having trusted personal
relationships with business owners, exploring
their goals and providing accountability &
advice to help them get Cashed Up.

Core Values

Dream Big

- Shoot for the moon.
- Challenge yourself and others to greatness.
- Step outside of your comfort zone and take a risk.
- Be creative - do something that wasn't asked of you, put yourself out on a limb.
- Step up and get better.

Make An Impact

- We're here to GSD or "get sh*t done".
- Make an impact and get results.
- Do meaningful work - you're not here to look good and go nowhere.
- Fulfil business and personal potential - be productive in all you do.

Remember Your Roots

- Wake up everyday and feel excited.
- BE the source of inspiration.
- Connect and communicate with everyone that touches the business.
- Inspire is a BS free zone. No politics. Zero bitching. Drama, gossip and moaning have no place here.

WHY WE EXIST

We are numbers people and we believe that FAMILY is number one. We exist to help Young Families use their Small Business to get Cashed Up.

OUR MISSION | We're on a mission to become Australia's Most Impactful Accounting firm. Ultimately it's about helping our clients pull more money, time and happiness from their business - measured in Freedom Days or Net Wealth / Cost of Living per Day. The 10 year vision is to give the proactive advice that helps create 10,000,000 Freedom Days, across 10 cities.

ENVIRONMENT
DICTATES PERFORMANCE

Dream Big. Make an Impact. Remember Your Roots.

This is our version of "How Sh*t Gets Done around Inspire." Unlike a traditional policy document, we wanted to be more human about things. We will have more formal policy documents which explain all the do's and don'ts in detail, but we think this is a great overview

The following 14 Agreements point to the fact that in business (and in life), all we can do is manage our agreements.

Marathons & Sprints.

Like Dog Years, a single year at Inspire could be likened to seven years in a more traditional firm. We run at a serious pace. To avoid burnout, we run our business to a "3 x 4" rhythm or 3 x 4 month quarters in a year instead of the traditional "4 x 3". Each quarter will have a clear theme and focus, and every team member will know their role to play, climaxing with a month of Celebration.

Celebrate	Activate	Recalibrate	Accelerate	Celebrate	Activate	Recalibrate	Accelerate	Celebrate	Activate	Recalibrate	Accelerate
Nov	Dec	Jan	Feb	Mar	Apr	May	Jun	Jul	Aug	Sep	Oct

Sharpening the axe.

Celebration months are a great opportunity for 'Service & Maintenance' as it's the only time that 'the speed train' - that is inspire - slows down long enough to onboard new team members, allow team to take a well earned holiday or do some epic personal and professional development. In November, March and July each year for example, we celebrate our wins with a 2 day offsite team retreat called Thinking and Thanking Day.

The Game Plan.

Like a team in a locker room moments before running onto the field, our retreats help every person on the team know exactly the role they each play in winning the game. Client Service

Coordinators, Account Managers, Business Development Managers and Quality Controllers, each have a different (but complementary) role to play for the quarter, summarised in one key Measure of Success. For example, "5 x Proactive Advice Meetings / week" or "5 x 2nd Opinions on Tax / week" when repeated 13 times over the 13 weeks in a quarter keeps us each 'on track' to win as a team. Because we are all dependant on each other, it's fine to be ahead, or on track but **it is not ok to be behind.**

Own the day.

To help you create space for personal or family success, we do an 'early start, early finish' with office hours between 7:20 and 3:50. Daily at 747 sharp we assemble in a circle for a Standing Team Huddle where we each share 3 things - What am I grateful for? What are my top 3 priorities for today? Am I ahead, on track or behind with my Measures of Success? Think of "747" as everyone standing around a campfire and the goal is to get everyone warmed up. What you say and how you say it can be like either throwing cold water or fuel on the fire. Please be brief, inspirational and to the point.

Get sh*t done.

Ever noticed how productive you are when you've worked either on an airplane, from home or at a cafe with your headphones on? *Distractions are the enemy of productivity.* That's why "747" is followed by 2 hours of GSD time - no emails, no client meetings, no phone calls and best of all, no one tapping you on the shoulder to ask a question, until 10 am. Seriously, unless there's a comet about to hit our office, don't bug anyone.

Batch-sh*t crazy.

The relentless pursuit of GSD also sees us 'batch' all our client meetings on Tuesday - Thursday, leaving Monday's & Friday's to prepare and follow up. It's also why we don't live in our inboxes. Emails are only 'let in' to our inbox 3 x times a day - thanks to a software called Boomerang.

Inbox Zero.

Everyday we achieve Inbox Zero. Every email in our inbox is either acknowledged or actioned on the day it's received. Most client emails are actually answered by our team of Client Service Coordinators and Junior Accountants. So it's just the curly ones that make it through to you. Inbox Zero helps us stay well within our promise to our clients of a "guaranteed 24 hour response to your questions, *or we'll send you a bunch of flowers*".

Gratitude is a gamechanger.

Every Friday morning we do Team Thankyou. A standing circle of gratitude where we THANK each other for the impact we've heard or seen each other make during the week.

There's laughter, there's smiles and sometimes even tears. Definitely the highlight of the week.

Deadlines become Lifelines.

Preparing Tax Returns & Financial Statements is like driving in a car looking through the rear vision mirror. While being compliant with the ATO is important, we ultimately want to help our clients make the 7 Smart Financial Decisions of a Cashed Up business. That's why we turn ATO Deadlines into Business Lifelines through early lodgment and proactive advice - this is like looking through the front windscreen, helping clients take the shortest and fastest route to their destination. For example –

- Quarterly BAS are finalised *2 weeks before* they're due, so clients have time to plan cashflow.

- Tax Planning is done with every client by May 15, so clients *still have 6 weeks* to implement before 30 June.

- We run an 'Annual General Meeting' with each of our clients when we finish their Tax Returns & Financial Statements in October, so they still have Nov - June to make this the best financial year yet.

Death before Timesheets.

You may know by now we don't do timesheets. So ... what do we measure then? *Impact.*

- Tax Savings
- Increases in Profit & Business Value & Wealth
- Reduction in Cashflow Days, Debt & Cost of Living.
- The ultimate impact is Freedom Days. which calculated by "Net Wealth / Cost of Living per Day" is really the sum of all these impacts combined.

At Inspire we believe that 'Advice Precedes Impact'. Instead of timesheets, everyday and every week we track the number of "Proactive Advice Meetings" we've delivered, then every quarter we measure the impact of our advice on our clients business and lives.

Communication over Calculation.

He who communicates best, wins. To date your career progression has been focused around upping your technical knowledge. From here on in it's about becoming a MASTER COMMUNICATOR. Knowing your sh*t is important, but that just gets you a foot in the door. "Making an impact", becoming a "Life Changing Accountant" and helping people get "Cashed Up" will require you to learn how to communicate in such a way that people listen, take action and leave feeling inspired.

Dress to Impress.

The dress code at Inspire is Super Smart Casual. We want to strike the fine balance between "I'm down to earth and approachable" and "I'm a qualified professional, ready to make an impact". You'll *never* see us in a suit or tie. Some cool jeans or a skirt with an Inspire T Shirt and a collared shirt over the top will do the trick. In short, we want people to judge us by the impact we make, not the clothes we wear. However we'd never want to dress in such a way that people find it hard to have *instant trust* in sharing with us their most intimate financial details.

Leave, leave, leave.

Annual Leave ...

Celebration months are a great time to take leave, but you're free to take annual leave whenever you like with plenty of notice. Just put your initials on the dates you're thinking of taking in the Activities Calendar. At our Quarterly Retreats we help you to plan your holidays a year in advance so you always have something to look forward to.

Sick Leave ...

If you're sick, you're sick. Just take the day off and get better. We'll see you again tomorrow, when you're 100%. I'm sure your emails and client meetings will still be there for you when you get back. No need to work from home.

I'm-not-really-feeling-it-so-I'm-working-from-home-or-leaving-early-leave ...

We're definitely not a team of clock-watchers, but out of respect for the team we are part of, we show up on time and ready to make an impact. We don't duck off early and there's not really a culture of working from home. We recognise that we are part of an inspirational team of game changers, and value the opportunity we have to work side by side with people we actually respect (and even love).

High-five the status quo in the face - with a chair.

We are best selling authors. We've won multiple awards. We regularly get invited to feature in the media and speak on business and personal success around Australia and internationally. Although we've just begun, we're already worthy of the title "Australia's Most Impactful Accounting Firm." None of which is possible without a culture of *extreme* innovation, profound rejection of the status quo and a strong desire for everyone to embrace change. **You up for the challenge?**

FROM COAL TO DIAMONDS

Dream Big. Make an Impact. Remember Your Roots.

Here's the essence of the 5 ish Year Plan to become a Life Changing Accountant.

- The goal is to become the Trusted Advisor to 50 x 6 & 7 Figure Businesses.
- Helping them make the 7 smart financial decisions of a Cashed Up business.
- Through 3 core services - Tax & Accounting, Business & Wealth Advisory.
- With the ultimate result of your advice being measured in Freedom Days - a day where you can do what you want, when you want, with whom you want.
- That's going to take some *serious* personal and professional development together.
- You'll learn (if you commit yourself) to do in 5 to 7 years, what partners of other Accounting firms do in an entire career.
- Just take that in for a minute [Deep Breathe IN ... and OUT]
- So let's get into it!
- Level 1, Junior Accountant - You master BAS, Xero, Tax Returns & Financial Statements and how to Offshore Jobs. We call this "Coal".
- Level 2, Junior Account Manager. You start building your own client base as you learn the Sales & Onboarding Process and get the ball rolling on your CA studies. We call this "Bronze".
- Level 3, Account Manager. You have your first 20 ish clients now. You're fairly competent a delivering Tax Planning, AGM's and SSS, *solo*. You're "Silver" and on between $50K and $65K.
- Level 4, Senior Account Manager. You're getting close to maxing out your clients. CA is almost done. And you're now starting to help your clients as

a CFO, not just as a tax agent. This is "Gold" and worth about $65k - $85k salary.

- Level 5, Team Leader. You no longer take on any new Inspire Family (except to replace any non-renewals). You lead a small team who assist you with delivering Tax, Accounting and Bookkeeping and in return you mentor them to become a Senior Account Manager. Most of your client focus is now high level business advice. You're a Tax Agent and as a "Platinum", you're earning $80-90K + a share of the profits your clients bring to Inspire.
- [Pause - Now this is where things get a little conceptual as we've not yet successfully mentored a team member to this point. So the follow is the gist of how we think things will pan out.]
- Level 6, "Business Leader". $130K plus a share of the profits that your clients and your team bring to Inspire. As a qualified Financial Planner, you've got the ability to give some high level wealth advice here too.
- Level 7, "City Leader". Think $200K plus profits. You're now like a fully fledged partner of an accounting firm, without all the risk and pain associated with building a business. In saying that you'd need to do something like an MBA to learn how to best keep leading the team / business forward.
- Level 8. Let's chat about this over a whiskey one time ...
- In summary.
- On our journey to becoming "Australia's Most Impactful Accounting Firm",
- Located in 10 cities and giving the advice that creates 10M Freedom Days
- and gives $1Bn to families in need.
- The ability for you to Dream Big, Make an Impact and Remember Your Roots,
- ... is endless.

That's the future. Some would call it pretty inspirational really.

So here's the series of steps we take week on week to get there.

- The goal is to just get 2 x NEW Inspire Family / month.
- While executing one of our 3 x Annual Campaigns.
- Except for during a Celebration Month in Mar, Jul & Nov.
- The Quarterly Campaigns are -

- Business Advisory & Financial Controls - Dec, Jan & Feb
- Proactive Tax Planning - Apr, May & Jun
- Annual General Meetings - Aug, Sep & Oct.
- We don't use timesheets at Inspire. *Thank god.*
- Instead we track Proactive Advice Meetings or PAM's.
- And every Account Manager's target is to deliver 5 x PAM's a week.
- If you're early in your 5 year plan, your PAM's will predominantly be made up of Sales, Onboarding and Production related PAM's.
- If you're later in your 5 year plan, your PAM's will predominantly be made up of Advice related PAM's - Tax Planning, AGM's and CFO meetings.
- Best of all, when we *all* hit our weekly PAM's (or Measures of Success MOS's for the non-accounting team) we get to leave the office at 12:30 on Fridays.
- Yes, this accountability does include Ben & Harvee too ...
- Afterall, we all equally rely on each other to succeed and make an impact.
- Put simply, success looks like 5 x PAM's a week and welcoming 6 x NEW Inspire Family / Quarter.
- FYI It takes about 2 x Look Under the Hood Delivery Meetings to get 1 x NEW Inspire Family member (aka a client) on board.
- And it takes about 6 x PAM's a year to deliver our "It's all sorted" | Tax & Accounting service, for each Inspire Family.
- Final note - PAM's won't fall on your lap each week.
- They're a result of *proactive* activity - whether it's processing jobs, following up on leads, chasing up checklists, clearing queries from Odyssey, asking clients for referrals, chasing the growth team for leads or bugging the workflow leader for jobs, to name a few.

Personal Growth comes before Professional Growth

- Every week we report in publically on our PAM's (or MOS) as a team.
- We also choose a personal goal to focus on in the quarter, and report on this each week too.
- At the end of every quarter we go offsite on a 2 day Team Retreat called a Thinking and Thanking Day.
- Day 1 is Personal Development. Day 2 is Professional Development.
- This is where the Performance and Salary Reviews happen, to track progress on our 5 Year Personal Business Plans.

- Every quarter we *each* read and implement a book from the required reading, to help accelerate our growth. That's 3 books / year.
- Monday's we have our Workflow and Opportunities meeting. These set the pace and scene for how to make this week GREAT.
- Friday's we have our Team Thankyou. This rounds off our week with a deep sense of gratitude and fulfillment, from what we've achieved this week.
- Daily we have a brief huddle at 747, called '747' to share our gratitude and top 3 priorities for the day.
- Because at the end of the day, a GREAT day makes a GREAT week.
- 52 GREAT weeks make a GREAT year.
- And 5 to 7 GREAT years and you've just completed a beautiful transformation from Coal through to Diamond.
- I'd love to leave you with an inspirational quote.
- *"A diamond is just a piece of coal, that did well under pressure."* Henry Kissinger

Please update Your Personal Business Plan & Inspire "CA" Learning and Development Plan.

What stage of the Coals to Diamond Journey are you at now?

What stage are you aiming towards?

By when?

And why do you want to be a [Insert Stage Name] at Inspire? Why does that excite you?

Which track are you aiming for this quarter?

5 x PAM's / Week - No Progress
6 x PAM's / Week - Slow Progress
7 x PAM's / Week - Average Progress
8 x PAM's / Week - Fast Progress
9 x PAM's / Week - Great Progress
10 x PAM's / Week - Accelerated Progress

1	2	3	4	5	6	7	8	9	10+
Inspire might not be the best place for you ... and that's ok. It's not for everyone.				No Progress	Slow Progress	Good Progress	Fast Progress	Great Progress	Accelerated Progress

How many PAM's are you aiming for this week?

7 / 5

How many did you hit last week? Why?

7 / 5

What's the mix between Workflow PAM's and Leadflow PAM's?

EVERYONE ROWING IN THE SAME
DIRECTION
Dream Big. Make an Impact. Remember Your Roots.

[Opener] Welcome to our Weekly Pulse – allow me to kick off this brief momentum session by reminding us all of some key principles –

We truly believe it when they say, *"If you could get all the people in the organization rowing in the same direction, you could dominate any industry, in any market, against any competition, at any time."*

So let's take a minute to refresh ourselves as leaders on exactly are we going …

The Grand Plan

Our Why – We are numbers people and we believe that family is number one. We help Young Families use their Small Business to get Cashed Up.

Our Mission – is to become "Australia's Most Impactful Accounting Firm", by giving the proactive advice that creates 10,000,000 Freedom Days.

Our Values – Dream Big. Make an Impact. Remember Your Roots.

Our 10 (ish) Year Vision – Inspire in 10 cities. Advice that creates 10M Freedom Days. Giving 1Bn Days of Life Changing help to end global poverty.

The 3 Year Plan – Inspire Brisbane. 12 x Life Changing Accountants. 50 x 6 & 7 figure businesses. 3 x Core Services (Tax, CFO & Wealth).

Our 10 Top New Year's Resolutions (2019 FY)

1. Destroy $140K Debt & Build $160K Rainy Day Fund.
2. Champion the Leadership Team.
3. Hire 4 x NEW Accountants (Mar & Jun 2019) & 2 x CSC's.
4. Track our first 100K Freedom Days
5. Hit 200 x Tax clients.
6. 50 x CFO clients.

7. 100 x Bookkeeping clients.
8. Fund $20M x Inspire Leverage.
9. Help our clients #BANK1MPROFIT.
10. Reach $15M Tax savings & Give 15M days of access to food, water, health & sanitation.

This leads into our Quarterly Rocks, which we'll cover in the SCORECARD shortly ...

So today we gather as a leadership team, once a week to take the pulse of our business. Reviewing 5 to 15 key numbers that let us know if we are -

- Ahead (Green)
- Behind (Orange) or
- Off-Track (Red)

In an environment where everyone is accountable, *all of the time,* we know that -

- What you can measure you can manage.
- What gets measured gets done.
- What gets measured get treasured.

So let us take the pulse of inspire,
by reviewing the Measures of Success | SCORECARD
and know that for every issue that arises,
together we have the answer.

Measures of Success | SCORECARD Update

Let's go top to bottom through the SCORECARD and brainstorm as a group (on the issues & opportunities list) what we need to do to turn the Reds into Oranges and the Oranges into Gre

21 Goals

The 7 Smart Financial Decisions of a Cashed Up Business

	Capture Profit	Control Cashflow		Grow Rev + Value	Cover Assets	Create Lifestyle

NOW	Where are you now vs where do you want to be?	FUTURE
	21 Goals to achieve in the next 3 years	
Paying Too Much Tax	Tax	Your Fair Share
	Days in Office (per week)	
	Business Revenue	
	Business Profit	
	Business Value	
	Size of Team	
	Giving to Charity	
	Personal Hobbies	
	Annual Family Holidays (weeks per year)	
	Dream Holiday Destination	
	Dream Holiday Destination	
	Dream Holiday Destination	
	Family Goals	
	Business Debt	
	Personal Debt	
	Family Home	
	Family Car	
	Investment - Property	
	Investment - Shares	
	Investment - Super	
	Anything Else?	

Money is not the most important thing in the world. However at some point in time, money is going to control where you live, what you eat and where you choose to holiday. So it is important to have a plan. A plan for how to pull more money out of your business, so that you can spend more time with your family and enjoy doing the things you love to do.

We help Young Families Use Their Small Business to get **Cashed Up.**

inspire™

21 Key Learnings from the
2 HR CASHED UP WORKSHOP

SAVE TAX, BOOST PROFITS & ACCELERATE CASHFLOW

21 Key Learnings from the
2 HR CASHED UP WORKSHOP
SAVE TAX, BOOST PROFITS & ACCELERATE CASHFLOW

Dream Big. Make an Impact. Remember Your Roots.

The dust has well and truly settled and I'm sure we are all back into the craziness that is our daily life. Thank you so much for letting us guide you through the 2 HR CASHED UP Workshop, I loved every minute.

Please find below 21 x Key Learnings from the Cashed Up Workshop.

And I'm also loving seeing some of you add me on instagram @HarveePene and sharing your experiences.

Please do keep in touch!

Harvee Pene
Author, TEDx Speaker & Co-Founder of Inspire - Life Changing Accountants

1 - Inspire before you Expire. If today was your last day, would you be happy with what you left behind?

2 - Family. Your Most Important Business. Knowing your WHY in Business can be as important as Knowing your NUMBERS. Business is Tough. "Business is a walk in the park ... JURASSIC PARK!" If you want to go the distance, make it through the hard times and get Cashed Up, your WHY is what will get you through. What is your why?

3 - Life Changing Accountants.

We set out on a mission to become AU most Impactful Accounting Firm - proud to say as of today we've proactively saved our small business clients over $9M+ in Tax, which they use to reinvest back into growing their business and family.

4 - Day for Dollar. See image.

5 - Purpose Beyond Profits. "When a business has no purpose other than to succeed financially, everyone involved adopts the same mentality. Customers only buy for their personal financial gain, employees work only for financial rewards and investors only inject funds in the hope of a quick return.

This probably doesn't cause a problem if everyone is making money but if ever the tide turns for just a short time, everyone runs for the exit." Daniel Priestley

6 - The Cashed Up Scorecard. 40 x priorities to kickstart your Cashed Up journey. This is both a master to do list for you over the next 3 to 5 years, but also an idea of the types of smart financial decisions that a Life Changing Accountant can help you and your family to make.

7 - Four Types of Wealth - 1. Financial Wealth (Money). 2. Social Wealth (Family & Friends). 3. Physical Wealth (Health). 4. Time Wealth (Freedom). Beware of making Money, at the cost of your Family, Friends, Health & Time. "A business that makes nothing but money is a poor business." Henry Ford.

8 - Respect PARKINSONS LAW! An available resource will always be used up e.g. Time - 'if it's available, we'll use it', e.g. Food - 'if it's there, we'll eat it', e.g. Money - if it's there, we'll spend it'.

9 - Freedom Days = $Net Wealth / Cost of Living Per Day, measures true wealth based on the philosophy that what makes us truly rich is the time we have on this earth, not the money we have in our accounts.

10 - "Sales - Profit = Expenses", means that a small percentage of every dollar that comes in the door, first gets squirreled away into your Profit War Chest. For more advanced application of this formula, I recommend reading the book Profit First by Mike Michalowicz.

11 - Tax War Chest. Many business owners complain when they get a surprise bill from the ATO. So a Cashed Up business utilises a Tax War Chest to squirrel money away for PAYG, GST & Tax, so they can pay their ATO bills in full and on time.

4 TYPES OF WEALTH

12 - Is your Accountant a Dinosaur?

Charge by hour.	You push them.
Not proactive.	Not entrepreneurial.
Surprise bills.	$$ to ask questions.
Slow to respond.	No Tax Savings
Just do tax.	If any of this sounds
Not tech savvy.	familiar to you ...

It might be time to Change Accountants?

13 - Power of Compounding.

What's $1.00 doubled 20x Times? So we'd go from $1 to $2 to $4 to $8 to $16 to $32 to $64 etc ... and do that 20x times. And we get a massive $1,048,576.00! But what would happen if we taxed this magic of compounding at just 25%. So we'd go $1 to $2, less $0.25 = $1.75. Do that twenty times and you're left with just $72,570.64.

That's why it's impossible to get Cashed Up, if you're giving half your profits to the tax man!

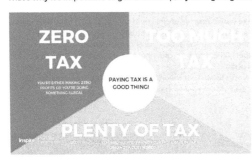

14 - Zero Tax? Too Much Tax? Plenty of Tax? Finding ways to avoid paying tax is almost an Australian sport. And I get it, the tax man doesn't deserve a tip. But paying tax is actually a good thing! If you're paying ZERO TAX it means you're either making no profit or you're doing something illegal. If you're paying TOO MUCH TAX it means you're probably giving the tax man a tip, because your current accountant is a dinosaur. Ultimately, you want to pay PLENTY OF TAX because it means you're making great profits, and you're paying your fair share in Tax ... and not a cent more.

15 - Trusts vs Company vs Sole Trader. On this journey called Entrepreneur-SHIP there are 3 different types of business structures or 'boats' that can help you make this journey. The correct use of business structures has been responsible for our almost $10M+ in proactive tax savings for our small business clients.

16 - The Million Dollar Pharmacist. Remember the Pharmacist who ran 2x multimillion dollar pharmacies AND owned the buildings in which they operated. And we was a Sole Trader! Giving half his profits to the tax man. Having almost ZERO ability to legally reduce his tax. And having ALL his hard earned assets on the line. The wasn't a warning lesson about business structures, but rather about dinosaur accountants.

17 - A Family Trust is like a Jug. We love Discretionary Trusts, because they give us the 'discretion' about who pays the tax & when. The idea: distribute the profits to family members & entities who pay tax at a lower rate than if you were a sole trader paying tax at about 50%.

18 - Never, ever, ever operate as a Sole Trader.

19 - Advanced SMSF Strategy No. 1 - Saving $96,000 a year by buying our Commercial Premises (Inspire HQ) in our Family SMSF.

We used to have a commercial lease of $12,500 + GST per month, until we bought and renovated a 200 sqm office in Fortitude Valley (1 km from Brisbane CBD) using our SMSF. My company Inspire CA now rents our office from our Family SMSF, at a 10% return for the SMSF, saving $96,000 a year for my company and 100% of the strategy is building my family wealth.

20 - Advanced SMSF Strategy No. 2 - Paying $0 Tax on $4M+ Profit. I used to not like Super because as a 30 year old it felt like it was 'forever' until I could access it. But then I learned about Parkinsons Law and realised that for me a SMSF is actually a beautiful "Retirement War Chest" - separate account, separate bank & difficult to access. For example, did you know there are 2 tax rates in Super? 15% while it's 'growing' aka in accumulation phase. 0% while it is 'going' aka in pension phase. So let's say we sell the Inspire office (owned by the SMSF) in 30 years time, and it's worth $5M. That means I can earn a $4M Profit and pay $0 Tax, legally. Imagine paying tax on $4M+ in your own name!

Inspire Office - Before   Inspire Office - After

Inspire Office - During

21 - There's 6 different ways you can pay yourself, but only 1 right way for you and your business.

In a Company you can pay yourself a Salary, a Loan (Division 7a) or a Dividend. In a Trust you can you yourself a Salary, a Loan (Drawings) or Distributions. Make sure you're pulling money out of your business the right way or risk paying thousands in excess tax.

10 DISTRIBUTION TARGETS

TARGET	WATCH FOR
1. You	$90k limit
2. Your spouse	Other income, HECS
3. Your retired parents	Self-Funded & Other income
4. Your children	Max $416 if under 18, HECS if over
5. Your siblings	Other income, HECS, Family Tax Benefits
6. Grandparents	Self-Funded & Other income
7. Superannuation	Contribution Caps
8. Church / Charity	Income tax exemption
9. Loss making business	Family Trust Election
10. Bucket company	All other income

- SALARY (PAYGW & SUPER)
- LOAN (DIV 7A)

COMPANY
- DIVIDEND

TRUST
- SALARY (PAYG & SUPER)
- LOAN (DRAWINGS)
- DISTRIBUTIONS

6 WAYS TO PULL MONEY OUT OF YOUR BUSINESS

inspire | LIFE CHANGING ACCOUNTANTS

PAY YOUR FAIR SHARE OF TAX
& NOT A CENT MORE!

GOT A FEELING YOU'RE PAYING TOO MUCH TAX OR THAT IT'S TIME TO CHANGE ACCOUNTANTS & FINALLY GET CASHED UP?

Look Under the Hood: $500 2nd Opinion on Tax, guaranteed to find $500 in Tax Savings or it's free. We usually find $600 to $60,000 in Tax Savings, which we call your MAGIC NUMBER, so you really have nothing to lose!

Bonus for Prompt Action: The first to submit this form will receive 2 x tickets for YOU + A GUEST to the 8 HR Profit Acceleration Workshop "Get Profit" covering the 5 P's of Profit - Psychology, Priority, Predictability, Protection & Purpose, valued at $500 each.

Next Steps to get the ball rolling: Submit this form, and then *all we need are Your Most Recent Tax Returns & Financial Statements that your accountant has prepared for your family & business.* We'll get back to you in 48 hours with a 'magic number' of tax savings other opportunities we've found for you to Save Tax, Boost Profits & Accelerate Cashflow.

And for every dollar in Tax Savings that we find you, on your behalf, we'll give that many days of access to Food, Water, Health our Sanitation to a family in need. $5,000 Tax Savings = $5,000 Days of Life Changing Help to End Global Poverty.

PAYMENT TYPE (tick one)   Visa ☐   Mastercard ☐   AMEX ☐

☐ $500+GST (GUARANTEED $500 IN TAX SAVINGS OR THIS WILL BE REFUNDED TO YOU)

Your Name   . . . .

Name on Card   . . . .

Card No.   ☐☐☐☐ ☐☐☐☐ ☐☐☐☐ ☐☐☐☐

Security Code ☐☐☐☐   Expiry Date   . . . . / . . . .

Signature

(Please take a photo of this form, your tax receipt will be sent within hours)   *Prices ex. GST

WANNA GO ON A DATE?

Thinking of Changing Accountants? Let's just take it easy and go on a few dates first to see if each other is 'the one'.

FIRST DATE

Learn about the 7 Smart Financial Decisions of a Cashed Up Business by Ben Walker & Harvee Pene with the **Cashed Up Book, Workshop & Scorecard.**

SECOND DATE

Let's take the next step by doing a **"Look Under the Hood"**. A $500 2nd Opinion on Tax, guaranteed to find $500 in tax savings or it's free.

THIRD DATE

Let's complete an "Urgent Need" project upfront to help claw back $$$'s in overpaid tax, get up to date with the ATO and / or set up NEW business structures.

THE PROPOSAL

We invite less than 50% of the Businesses we meet to become a client - or what we call 'join the Inspire Family'. To receive an invitation we need to know -

1 - Is there potential to ADD MASSIVE VALUE TO YOUR BUSINESS?
2 - Do we SHARE COMMON VALUES?
3 - How will you use your BUSINESS FOR GOOD?

IT'S ALL SORTED

Proactive Tax & Accounting that pays for itself in Tax Savings (av. 4 x ROI) & a Life Changing Accountant that you see 4 x times a year, to help you make Smart Financial Decisions. Starts at $600 / month + GST.

TOTAL FINANCIAL CONTROL

Proactive Financial Co-Pilot (Business) to help you Work 4 Days a Week, 40 Weeks a Year & Pull $400K+ Profit per Year. Starts at $600 / month + GST.

THE GOOD LIFE

Proactive Financial Co-Pilot (Personal) to help you Build $4M+ in 4 Pools of Wealth to Last 4 Generations. Starts at $600 / month + GST.

inspire.business   1300 852 747   hello@inspireca.com

DREAM BIG
MAKE AN
IMPACT
REMEMBER YOUR ROOTS

LIFE CHANGING ACCOUNTANTS

inspire™

A bit about us ...

We are www.inspireca.com

We're a team of Accountants and numbers people who believe that Family is number one.

We're best known for having proactively saved our 6 & 7 figure business clients $3M+ in tax.

Best of all, for every dollar of tax we save a small business, Inspire provides a days access to food, water, health and sanitation to families in need.

We help business owners keep more of their hard earned cash in 2 ways -

1. Our award winning proactive tax & accounting service - called "It's all sorted" - pays for itself in tax savings. On average we've saved our clients $18,000 / year, which is 3x what they pay us (about $500 / month).

2. Our well known 2nd Opinion on Tax service - called "Look Under the Hood" is $500 and guarantees to find $500 in tax savings or it's free. Business owners usually get a 2nd Opinion before they become a client of It's all sorted.

In the last 5 years we've built a decent business ourselves with offices in Brisbane, Sydney and Melbourne since dropping out of the Big 4 and starting Inspire with nothing but a laptop, a borrowed printer and a dream.

Our head office is in Brisbane with a growing team of 6 Accountants, 2 Junior Accountants, 2 client service coordinators and an offshore processing team in Vietnam - plus the 2 founders Ben Walker & Harvee Pene.

One of our founders spoke at TEDx on achieving big goals, the other has won a number of awards in entrepreneurship and together they are the authors of the book Cashed Up - 7 steps to pull more money, time and happiness from your business. They've also co-authored Better Business, Better Life, Better World and are featured in "The World's Most Inspirational Accountants" by Steve Pipe. Pretty inspirational guys...

We've won numerous awards, have partnered with organisations like Commonwealth Bank, Westpac, Xero and regularly feature in the media and on industry podcasts (just quietly).

We're known for Helping Young Families Use their Small Business to get Cashed Up and our mission is to become *Australia's Most Impactful Accounting Firm*. We've not only proactively saved our clients $3M in Tax but their revenues and profits have grown by 149% and 47% respectively.

And thanks to our Day for a Dollar campaign, we've given 3M+ days worth of access to water, food, health and sanitation to families in need across 16 countries...

Ultimately, we exist to help our clients build businesses that give them the freedom to put family first and make a difference in the world. It's a pretty inspiring place to work actually.

A bit about the role ...

Firstly let's get the money out of the way. $65 - $80K with plenty of room to grow.

The essence of the role is simple -

Help us *dramatically* grow the 'Inspire Family' nationwide, developing trusted personal relationships with business owners, exploring their goals, solving their problems and set them on the path to getting Cashed Up.

Really it's about selling the "BIG PICTURE" then selling the "NEXT STEP".

Sell the "BIG PICTURE"

I believe that we were put on this earth to do more than break even. The problem is, the numbers tell us that businesses are struggling (ABS stats) -

- 2.1 Million Businesses in Australia.
- 90% of businesses are *small business*.
- 60% make less than $200k, aren't profitable, lose money or can't afford team.
- ¼ took on debt, did so for survival.
- ⅗ of all businesses won't survive 4 years.

Success in business is a series of smart financial decisions. In our book, we outline the 7 smart financial decisions of a Cashed Up Business. More about them later but in essence, business is a numbers game. The winners in the game of business know their numbers. Most business owners aren't numbers people and most accountants aren't business people. Enter Inspire ...

We're here to help Young Families use their Small Business to get Cashed Up. That means helping keep our 6 & 7 figure business owners ACCOUNT-able (the origins of the word accountant) to taking *'the 7 steps to pull more money time and happiness from your business'*.

Sell the 'Next Step'

"It's impossible to get Cashed Up, if you're giving half your profits to the tax man."

Everyone pays tax. But hidden within the tax we all pay, is tax we don't need to pay. The only way to tell the difference between the two is with a proactive accountant. Trouble is most accountants aren't proactive. Enter Inspire.

We've saved our small business clients 3M+ in tax, and our award winning core product – "It's all sorted" – pays for itself in tax savings.

Once someone is on board with the 'bigger picture' the next step is to solve an "Urgent Need". A small initial project to deliver a 'quick win' and help us figure out whether we're a good fit for eachother.

Our next steps or as we call them "Products for Prospects".

- ($500) Look Under the Hood - 2nd Opinion on your tax & your accountant, guaranteed to find $500 in tax savings or it's free.

- ($500) Structures & Strategies Session - Business Structuring Advice to save tax and protect assets, guaranteed to find $500 in tax savings or it's free.

- ($500) Where's your tax at? - Detailed Plan of Attack on how to get multiple years of outstanding tax obligations up to date (in 10 days) and the Tax Man off your back. $500 refunded / credited if you go ahead with the action plan.

Your Measures of Success will be -

- 25 Calls a Day.
- Sell 5 - 7x Products for Prospects a week.
- Maintain 'flow' of Sales Pipeline to deliver $20K cash / week.
- 2 x NEW 'Inspire Family' / Account Manager / Month.

Here's the typical sales flow -

1. A business owner will reach out to us wanting a 2nd Opinion on their Tax after -
   a. Reading our Cashed Up Book
   b. Attending the Save Tax Workshop or
   c. Being referred by a current client.
2. You'll have a quick chat (under 20 mins) on the phone to sell BIG PICTURE & assess -
   a. Years in business
   b. Current revenue & profit
   c. Current business structure (Sole Trader, Company or Trust)
   d. How they feel about tax? (Typically annoyed they're paying too much)

    e. How they feel about current accountant? (Typically annoyed because they are reactive)

    f. Willingness to invest in NEXT STEP (Typically a $500, 2nd Opinion on Tax, guaranteed to save $500 in tax savings or its free)

3. Coordinate information from the business owner and handover to Accountant to prepare 2nd Opinion.
4. Delivery Meeting with you and the Accountant - You start the online / in person meeting by introducing yourself, the accountant & inspire. Accountant educates the client on the tax saving strategies & advises (aka sells) an "Urgent Need" project that will trigger a refund of tax savings / urgent catch up of outstanding taxes. Typically $1,500 - $5,000 plus GST.
5. Accountant delivers "Urgent Need" in 10 business days, while business owner reviews -
    a. "What you can expect from US?" Please read.
    b. "What we expect from YOU?" Please read.
6. Assess whether they are suitable to join the Inspire Family -
    a. Can we confidently save them 2 - 3x in tax, what they're going to pay for It's all sorted?
    b. Are they going to be a headache or a dream to work with?
    c. Would we happily invite them and their family over for family dinner?
7. Delivery Meeting with you and the Accountant called "21 Goals". a 3 year goal setting workshop to help business owners get clear on what they want to achieve in their business, family and life. Demonstrates how having a 'trusted advisor' who keeps them accountable to the 7 smart financial decisions of a Cashed Up business, will help them make those goals a reality.
8. They accept a proposal for "It's all sorted" and typically pay $1,500 - $5,000 plus GST pro-rata (depending on the time of the year) and $500 / month ongoing.

So, how do you make the $20K weekly cash target?

- 5 x P4P's = 5 x $500 plus GST = $2,500
- 3 x Urgent Needs - 3 x $3,000 = $9,000
- 2 x Business Structure Set Ups - 2 x $2,000 = $4,000
- 3 x Upfront Joining Fees (Pro-rata) - 3 x $2,000 = $6,000

Total - $21,500 plus GST.

P.s. this is a pretty common week for us. It just relies on leads consistently coming through the front end and to work in with the accountants to maintain flow through the stages.

The context -

- We currently have about 100 x 6 & 7 figure businesses and
- 6 x Life Changing Accountants.
- Each accountant has the capacity to look after 50 x business clients.
- We're taking on just 12 x Accountants for Brisbane in 2018 & 19.
- So our capacity for Inspire Brisbane is 600 x Business clients.
- Our 3 year plan is to get Inspire Brisbane to capacity.
- Then (with your help) open Inspire Sydney & Inspire Melbourne. That's 1,800 businesses in the next 5 - 7 years.
- We take on clients according to our team capacity, which is 2 x NEW Inspire Family per Accountant per month.
- We've spent years systemising -
    - the business (Inspire Life Changing Accountants)
    - the core product ("It's all sorted" & the Cashed Up journey) and
    - the assets (Book, Look Under the Hood, Scripts, Product Brochures, Collateral etc
- It's ready to scale ... *with your help.*

And finally,

A bit about you ...

- You're a great communicator and people's person.
- You just want to help people, any way you can.
- You prefer small dynamic teams to being a cog in a big machine.
- You're honest and want to do the right thing by people.
- You're on a mission in life.
- You're great at communicating complex ideas, making them simple.
- You love to speak - over the phone, online and to groups of 10 - 50.
- You thrive on adding value to people and surprising them with "WOW" experiences.
- You don't mind expressing yourself.

- You can speak to other human beings about business, life, family and ... anything really.
- You take pride in your team and their achievements.
- You have high standards and thrive on accountability.
- You've got experience in the mechanics of running a business and can empathise with how tough business really is.
- You're observant. Your attention to detail allows you to stay one step ahead in preempting and solving problems as well as identifying and harnessing opportunities.
- You've got a big heart.
- You love a good laugh, a good feed and to travel.
- You love your family.
- You love doing good.
- You get the whole personal development thing and are an avid reader.
- You love a challenge.

The Prize

In the coming years we're poised to expand to new cities, roll out new service offerings - bookkeeping, business advisory & wealth, expand the team and triple our impact.

In the next 3 years, thanks to our Day for a Dollar Campaign, we're on track to hit $15M in tax savings and that sees us giving 15M days of access to life changing help. (Goodbye extreme global poverty!)

We've even had a game changing acquisition offer from one of our business idols who says we could partner with them to roll out Inspire globally. (Dibs on Inspire New York!)

So we're looking for a remarkable human who doesn't settle for the status quo and wants to lean in to a role that gives them a chance to dream big, make an impact and remember their roots.

Contact harvee@inspireca.com or 0422 845 277 to express why this excites you.

inspire™

POSITION DESCRIPTION

Business Development Manager or "BDM"

Dramatically grow the 'Inspire Family' nationwide, develop trusted personal relationships with business owners, exploring their goals, solving their problems and getting them on the path to getting Cashed Up.

Join the inspirational team that's been featured in -

A bit about us ...

We are www.inspireca.com

We're a team of Accountants and numbers people who believe that Family is number one.

We're best known for having proactively saved our 6 & 7 figure business clients $3M+ in tax.

Best of all, for every dollar of tax we save a small business, Inspire provides a days access to food, water, health and sanitation to families in need.

We help business owners keep more of their hard earned cash in 2 ways -

1. Our award winning proactive tax & accounting service - called "It's all sorted" - pays for itself in tax savings. On average we've saved our clients $18,000 / year, which is 3x what they pay us (about $500 / month).

2. Our well known 2nd Opinion on Tax service - called "Look Under the Hood" is $500 and guarantees to find $500 in tax savings or it's free. Business owners usually get a 2nd Opinion before they become a client of It's all sorted.

In the last 5 years we've built a decent business ourselves with offices in Brisbane, Sydney and Melbourne since dropping out of the Big 4 and starting Inspire with nothing but a laptop, a borrowed printer and a dream.

Our head office is in Brisbane with a growing team of 6 Accountants, 2 Junior Accountants, 2 client service coordinators and an offshore processing team in Vietnam - plus the 2 founders Ben Walker & Harvee Pene.

One of our founders spoke at TEDx on achieving big goals, the other has won a number of awards in entrepreneurship and together they are the authors of the book Cashed Up - 7 steps to pull more money, time and happiness from your business. They've also co-authored Better Business, Better Life, Better World and are featured in "The World's Most Inspirational Accountants" by Steve Pipe. Pretty inspirational guys...

We've won numerous awards, have partnered with organisations like Commonwealth Bank, Westpac, Xero and regularly feature in the media and on industry podcasts (just quietly).

We're known for Helping Young Families Use their Small Business to get Cashed Up and our mission is to become **Australia's Most Impactful Accounting Firm**. We've not only proactively saved our clients $3M in Tax but their revenues and profits have grown by 149% and 47% respectively.

And thanks to our Day for a Dollar campaign, we've given 3M+ days worth of access to water, food, health and sanitation to families in need across 16 countries...

Ultimately, we exist to help our clients build businesses that give them the freedom to put family first and make a difference in the world. It's a pretty inspiring place to work actually.

A bit about the role ...

Firstly let's get the money out of the way. $65 - $80K with plenty of room to grow.

The essence of the role is simple -

Help us *dramatically* grow the 'Inspire Family' nationwide, developing trusted personal relationships with business owners, exploring their goals, solving their problems and set them on the path to getting Cashed Up.

Really it's about selling the "BIG PICTURF" then selling the "NEXT STEP".

Sell the "BIG PICTURE"

I believe that we were put on this earth to do more than break even. The problem is, the numbers tell us that businesses are struggling (ABS stats) –

- 2.1 Million Businesses in Australia.
- 90% of businesses are *small business*.
- 60% make less than $200k, aren't profitable, lose money or can't afford team.
- ¼ took on debt, did so for survival.
- ⅗ of all businesses won't survive 4 years.

Success in business is a series of smart financial decisions. In our book, we outline the 7 smart financial decisions of a Cashed Up Business. More about them later but in essence, business is a numbers game. The winners in the game of business know their numbers. Most business owners aren't numbers people and most accountants aren't business people. Enter Inspire …

We're here to help Young Families use their Small Business to get Cashed Up. That means helping keep our 6 & 7 figure business owners ACCOUNT-able (the origins of the word accountant) to taking *'the 7 steps to pull more money time and happiness from your business'.*

Sell the 'Next Step'

"It's impossible to get Cashed Up, if you're giving half your profits to the tax man."

Everyone pays tax. But hidden within the tax we all pay, is tax we don't need to pay. The only way to tell the difference between the two is with a proactive accountant. Trouble is most accountants aren't proactive. Enter Inspire.

We've saved our small business clients 3M+ in tax, and our award winning core product – "It's all sorted" – pays for itself in tax savings.

Once someone is on board with the 'bigger picture' the next step is to solve an "Urgent Need". A small initial project to deliver a 'quick win' and help us figure out whether we're a good fit for eachother.

Our next steps or as we call them "Products for Prospects".

- ($500) Look Under the Hood - 2nd Opinion on your tax & your accountant, guaranteed to find $500 in tax savings or it's free.

- ($500) Structures & Strategies Session - Business Structuring Advice to save tax and protect assets, guaranteed to find $500 in tax savings or it's free.

- ($500) Where's your tax at? - Detailed Plan of Attack on how to get multiple years of outstanding tax obligations up to date (in 10 days) and the Tax Man off your back. $500 refunded / credited if you go ahead with the action plan.

Your Measures of Success will be -

- 25 Calls a Day.
- Sell 5 - 7x Products for Prospects a week.
- Maintain 'flow' of Sales Pipeline to deliver $20K cash / week.
- 2 x NEW 'Inspire Family' / Account Manager / Month.

Here's the typical sales flow -

1. A business owner will reach out to us wanting a 2nd Opinion on their Tax after -
   a. Reading our Cashed Up Book
   b. Attending the Save Tax Workshop or
   c. Being referred by a current client.
2. You'll have a quick chat (under 20 mins) on the phone to sell BIG PICTURE & assess -
   a. Years in business
   b. Current revenue & profit
   c. Current business structure (Sole Trader, Company or Trust)
   d. How they feel about tax? (Typically annoyed they're paying too much)

e. How they feel about current accountant? (Typically annoyed because they are reactive)
f. Willingness to invest in NEXT STEP (Typically a $500, 2nd Opinion on Tax, guaranteed to save $500 in tax savings or its free)

3. Coordinate information from the business owner and handover to Accountant to prepare 2nd Opinion.
4. Delivery Meeting with you and the Accountant - You start the online / in person meeting by introducing yourself, the accountant & inspire. Accountant educates the client on the tax saving strategies & advises (aka sells) an "Urgent Need" project that will trigger a refund of tax savings / urgent catch up of outstanding taxes. Typically $1,500 - $5,000 plus GST.
5. Accountant delivers "Urgent Need" in 10 business days, while business owner reviews -
   a. "What you can expect from US?" Please read.
   b. "What we expect from YOU?" Please read.
6. Assess whether they are suitable to join the Inspire Family -
   a. Can we confidently save them 2 - 3x in tax, what they're going to pay for It's all sorted?
   b. Are they going to be a headache or a dream to work with?
   c. Would we happily invite them and their family over for family dinner?
7. Delivery Meeting with you and the Accountant called "21 Goals". a 3 year goal setting workshop to help business owners get clear on what they want to achieve in their business, family and life. Demonstrates how having a 'trusted advisor' who keeps them accountable to the 7 smart financial decisions of a Cashed Up business, will help them make those goals a reality.
8. They accept a proposal for "It's all sorted" and typically pay $1,500 - $5,000 plus GST pro-rata (depending on the time of the year) and $500 / month ongoing.

So, how do you make the $20K weekly cash target?

- 5 x P4P's = 5 x $500 plus GST = $2,500
- 3 x Urgent Needs - 3 x $3,000 = $9,000
- 2 x Business Structure Set Ups - 2 x $2,000 = $4,000
- 3 x Upfront Joining Fees (Pro-rata) - 3 x $2,000 = $6,000

Total - $21,500 plus GST.

P.s. this is a pretty common week for us. It just relies on leads consistently coming through the front end and to work in with the accountants to maintain flow through the stages.

The context -

- We currently have about 100 x 6 & 7 figure businesses and
- 6 x Life Changing Accountants.
- Each accountant has the capacity to look after 50 x business clients.
- We're taking on just 12 x Accountants for Brisbane in 2018 & 19.
- So our capacity for Inspire Brisbane is 600 x Business clients.
- Our 3 year plan is to get Inspire Brisbane to capacity.
- Then (with your help) open Inspire Sydney & Inspire Melbourne. That's 1,800 businesses in the next 5 - 7 years.
- We take on clients according to our team capacity, which is 2 x NEW Inspire Family per Accountant per month.
- We've spent years systemising -
  - the business (Inspire Life Changing Accountants)
  - the core product ("It's all sorted" & the Cashed Up journey) and
  - the assets (Book, Look Under the Hood, Scripts, Product Brochures, Collateral etc
- It's ready to scale ... **with your help.**

And finally,

A bit about you ...

- You're a great communicator and people's person.
- You just want to help people, any way you can.
- You prefer small dynamic teams to being a cog in a big machine.
- You're honest and want to do the right thing by people.
- You're on a mission in life.
- You're great at communicating complex ideas, making them simple.
- You love to speak - over the phone, online and to groups of 10 - 50.
- You thrive on adding value to people and surprising them with "WOW" experiences.
- You don't mind expressing yourself.

- You can speak to other human beings about business, life, family and ... anything really.
- You take pride in your team and their achievements.
- You have high standards and thrive on accountability.
- You've got experience in the mechanics of running a business and can empathise with how tough business really is.
- You're observant. Your attention to detail allows you to stay one step ahead in preempting and solving problems as well as identifying and harnessing opportunities.
- You've got a big heart.
- You love a good laugh, a good feed and to travel.
- You love your family.
- You love doing good.
- You get the whole personal development thing and are an avid reader.
- You love a challenge.

The Prize

In the coming years we're poised to expand to new cities, roll out new service offerings - bookkeeping, business advisory & wealth, expand the team and triple our impact.

In the next 3 years, thanks to our Day for a Dollar Campaign, we're on track to hit $15M in tax savings and that sees us giving 15M days of access to life changing help. (Goodbye extreme global poverty!)

We've even had a game changing acquisition offer from one of our business idols who says we could partner with them to roll out Inspire globally. (Dibs on Inspire New York!)

So we're looking for a remarkable human who doesn't settle for the status quo and wants to lean in to a role that gives them a chance to dream big, make an impact and remember their roots.

Contact harvee@inspireca.com **or 0422 845 277 to express why this excites you.**

inspire™ | LIFE CHANGING ACCOUNTANTS

PARTNERSHIP OPPORTUNITY

COLLABORATION
OVER COMPETITION

*"if you want to go fast, go alone. If you want to go far, **go together**."*

Join the inspirational team that's been featured in -

COMPANY OVERVIEW

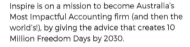 **inspire™** | LIFE CHANGING ACCOUNTANTS

We are numbers people and we believe FAMILY IS NUMBER ONE. We help Young Families use their Small Business to get **Cashed Up**.

Inspire is on a mission to become Australia's Most Impactful Accounting firm (and then the world's!), by giving the advice that creates 10 Million Freedom Days by 2030.

We're well known for proactively saving our 6 & 7 figure business clients over $7M in tax and giving 7 million days of life changing help to end extreme global poverty to families in need, across 16 countries.

WELL KNOWN AS -

- Authors of CASHED UP, 7 steps to pull more money, time and happiness from your business.
- Top 100 Companies in Australia (2017 & 2018).
- Accountants for Good - for every dollar of tax saved, inspire gives a days access to food, water, health and sanitation to help end global poverty.
- Trusted advisors to hundreds of 6 & 7 figure businesses owners across Brisbane, Sydney & Melbourne.

Dream Big. Make an Impact. Remember Your Roots.

What are all the different ways we could collaborate?

Here's an overview of our product ecosystem to get the creative juices flowing ...

Cashed Up Book | 7 steps to pull more money. time and happiness from your business.

Money is not the most important thing in the world. However at some point in time, money is going to control where you live, what you eat and where you choose to holiday.

So it is important to have a plan. A plan for how to pull more money out of your business, so that you can spend more time with your family and enjoy doing the things you love to do.

This book is your plan.

Cashed Up Scorecard | Benchmark your business against the 7 Smart Financial Decisions of a Cashed Up business.

The Cashed Up scorecard measures you against 7 Smart Financial Decisions of a Cashed Up business. Think of them as "priorities", vital to being able to pull more money, time and happiness from your business.

Take the Influence test and get a 20+ page report and complimentary book

Cashed Up Workshop | Free 2 HR Workshop for business owners to Save Tax, Boost Profits & Accelerate Cashflow.

You will learn:

* How to establish a Profit War Chest that guarantees you make a profit from your very next sale.
* How to get a firm grasp on the numbers so you don't run out of cash.
* How to stop giving half your profits to the taxman, without doing anything dodgy or illegal.

Hosted monthly in BNE, SYD & MEL.

Sponsorship Opportunities: Cross promotion of events, workshops, books, scorecards etc ...

More Money, Time & Happiness Conference - 2 day strategic business & lifestyle retreat to help business owners accelerate their Cashed Up Journey - 31 Oct & 1st Nov at Hilton Hotel Surfers Paradise

The goal of the conference is to help our 6 & 7 figure business clients make smarter financial decisions by introducing them to our partners in a value added way, and ultimately help them become clients of yours. This is a 'money-can't-buy' event. Our clients have to successfully refer / renew with us to get a seat at the table. We have space for 8 - 12 keynotes and a wish list of 25 speakers (below).

- Daniel & Justine Flynn, Thankyou - "Chapter One".
- Jeff Horne, Professional Boxer - "The Hornet"
- Taj Pabari, Young Australian of the Year - "LEVEL UP."
- Phillip Di Bella, Di Bella Coffee - "Entrepreneurial Intelligence."
- Paul Dunn & Masami Sato, B1G1 - "Better Life, Business & World."
- Ben Walker & Harvee Pene, Inspire - "Cashed Up".
- Glen Carlson, Dent Global - "Become a Key Person of Influence."
- Sarah Riegelhuth - "Get Rich Slow."
- Jon Hollenberg, Five by Five - "Love at First Site."
- Natasha Hawker, Employee Matters - "From Hire to Fire."
- Justine Coombe, Ignite Digital - "Conversion."
- Ronsley Vaz, Amplify Agency - "Amplify."

- Andrew Griffiths - "The Power of Publishing."
- Tim Reid, Small Business Big Marketing - "The Boomerang Effect."
- Kelvin Davis, Greymouse - "Accelerate Your Wealth."
- Dan Norris, Black Hops Brewery - "Create or Hate."
- Geoff Green, GRG Momentum - "The Smart Business Exit.
- David Dugan, Elite 500 - "Bullet Proof Business."
- Dale Beaumont, Business Blueprint - "Secrets of small business."
- Mandy Holloway, Courageous Leaders - "Inspiring Courageous Leaders."
- Jack Delosa, The Entourage - "Unprofessional."
- Petar Lackovic, The Entourage.
- Shane & Ange Saunders, Breathe Me, "How to lower stress, naturally."

Sponsorship Opportunities: Keynote, Promotion, Sponsorship ...

WE GIVE ONE DAY OF ACCESS TO FOOD, WATER, HEALTH OR SANITATION TO A FAMILY IN NEED, FOR EVERY DOLLAR IN TAX WE PROACTIVELY SAVE A SMALL BUSINESS.

DAYS OF LIFE CHANGING HELP GIVEN TO FAMILIES IN NEED TO END GLOBAL POVERTY

Inspiring Business for Good Podcast - inspiring stories and strategies of businesses that exist for Good. The good of the world, their clients, their team and their founders.

The goal is to deconstruct how inspirational business leaders (like yourself) make an impact, and ultimately prove that businesses who do good, do better.

Of course, this approach really helps the listener get what you do so hopefully will attract some opportunity. As well as inspire others to make a bigger impact.

It's an easy 40-ish minute audio only Skype interview that is recorded and aired through iTunes

What I'm about is really getting into the force multipliers, the high value / high impact stuff around -

- Effective Giving

- Business model design

- 'Vision, Mission & Values' led growth

- Impact at scale

- Revenue, Profit & Cash drivers

- Attracting top talent

- World class Leadership

- Leaving, Living and Leveraging a Legacy.

Because I believe that GOOD IS THE NEW GREAT ... and that in 2019+ if you aren't making an impact, you shouldn't be in business.

Sponsorship Opportunities: Interviews, Promotion, Sponsorship ...

Get
Cashed Up.

If you think it's about Tax & Accounting,
you've missed the point. it's about
pulling more money, time and
happiness out of your business.

inspire™   *"Top 100 Companies
in Australia"*

SPEAKERS KIT | HARVEE PENE - Author of Cashed Up, TEDx Speaker & Co-Founder of Inspire - Life Changing Accountants. One of Ten Outstanding Young Persons of Australia (2019) & Face of Movember

AUDIENCES HARVEE HAS SPOKEN FOR

"Harvee. Thank you very much for your time yesterday. You definitely left an imprint on the team and the themes you spoke about were so aligned to our day and where the team was at it was perfect. You made an impression on my leadership team so have no doubt you can for the state and excited to have you be apart of the ANZ family."

Lara Thomas. District Manager ANZ

HARVEE PENE | Cancer Survivor, Men's Health Ambassador & Face of MOVEMBER

"Inspired by our friends (and personal accountants) from inspire. This is the most inspiring accounting firm you will come across. Their vision and execution is world class. Watch this space."

Daniel Flynn, Co-Founder & MD Thankyou

ABOUT HARVEE PENE

Author, TEDx Speaker & Co-Founder of Inspire - Life
Changing Accountants.

ABOUT HARVEE PENE

Harvee Pene is co-founder of Inspire - Life Changing Accountants (Top 100
Companies in Australia - 2017 & 2018). He is a Business Advisor who helps
Young Families get Cashed Up, so they can use their **Business for Good.**

With more than 20 years business experience, he is the best selling author of
the books - **CASHED UP, LEGACY, 'BETTER BUSINESS BETTER LIFE, BETTER
WORLD' & 'GOOD IS THE NEW GREAT'.**

Believing that Good is the New Great, his Top 100 Australian podcast "Inspiring
Business for Good" showcases stories of Businesses that exist for the good of
their Founders, their Team, their Clients & the World.

At 31 years old Harvee was blindsided by Testicular Cancer. He healed himself
and is now a global ambassador for mens health with the MOVEMBER
Foundation. Feeling like he now has a second chance in life, he tries to live true
to his life's purpose - to **DO GOOD & INSPIRE OTHERS.**

As trusted advisor & accountants to the founders of Thankyou & ambassador for
Buy One Give One and the UN Global Goals, Harvee is on a mission to see the
end of extreme global poverty in his lifetime.

THE BOOK

Harvee launched his first book - co-authored with his best mate & business partner Ben Walker - in 2018 as a guide for business owners to pull **More Money, Time & Happiness from their Business.**

Harvee can include copies of the Cashed Up book as part of a speaking engagement package for your audience.

He can also arrange to be available for signing & photos after his talk.

CASHED UP

7 steps to pull more
money, time and happiness
from your business

Ben Walker & Harvee Pene

"If you're looking for ways to **Save Tax, Boost Profits & Accelerate your Cashflow,** then you definitely want to listen to Ben & Harvee!"

Glen Carlson, Co-Founder of Dent Global (Australia's 9th Fastest Growing Company)

THE TOP 100 PODCAST

Inspirational stories of businesses that exist for good - the good of their founders, their team, their clients and the world.

Harvee's goal is to deconstruct how business leaders make an impact and ultimately prove that **businesses who do good, do better.**

- Effective Giving and One for One.
- Business model design.
- Vision, Mission & Values led growth.
- Impact at scale.
- Revenue, Profit & Cashflow drivers.
- Attracting top talent.
- World class Leadership.
- And Leaving, Living and Leveraging a Legacy.

PJ Patterson on Leaving a Legacy & T
Inspiring Business for Good — 6 March

"Inspiring Business for Good is like sitting down & chatting with an amazing mentor over coffee each week. Harvee pulls out the gold from each person so that you can make the changes in your business "to inspire & do good." - **Emma Small**

GOOD IS THE NEW GREAT!

SPEAKER TOPIC 1

Spectacular proof that - "BUSINESSES DO GOOD, DO BETTER."

In a world where 796 Million People find themselves living in extreme global poverty (on about $1.25 per day), who is best to solve this global issue? Politicians? Celebrities? Governments? Churches?

What if the solution were to come from Entrepreneurs, the natural problem solvers? And what if doing good for the world, was also good for you, your team & your clients too?

"Never has there been a more exciting time for all of us to explore this next great frontier where the boundaries between work and higher purpose are merging into one, **where doing good really is good for business.**"

Sir Richard Branson, Virgin Group

STOP GIVING HALF YOUR PROFITS TO THE TAX MAN!

SPEAKER TOPIC 2

Think: Pauline Hanson. Barnaby Joyce. Senator Fraser Anning? When you think about these public servants, do you feel inspired to give them a tip?

It's impossible to get Cashed Up, if you're giving half your profits to the tax man!

So let's learn the strategies behind how we've been able to proactively save our small business clients $8M+ in tax & counting ...

"Epic Work: Trusts & Companies have been enigmatic to me for too long! The way you explained it, along with the common sense risk management is fantastic.;

Liz Kingston, Kingston Human Capital

BUILD YOUR PROFIT WAR CHEST

SPEAKER TOPIC 3

Ever noticed how no matter how much more you make, there never seems to be enough profit leftover?

Many growing businesses - regardless of size - suffer from a syndrome called "GROWING BROKE" where they find themselves making less and less profit on more and more income.

In a world where we tend to spend everything we earn, protecting your profit is vital.

You were put on this earth to do more than simply ... BREAK EVEN.

"Really great foundations to have a profitable business without sacrificing your passion."

Ale Wiecek, SQR One

GET **CASHED UP!**

SPEAKER TOPIC 4

Business in general is characterised by big winners and big loser but the majority of business owners exist between these two extremes, for better or worse.

Get Cashed Up is our guide to enabling business owners and their families to enjoy an extremely rewarding life, without living through uncomfortable extremes.

Jam packed full of strategies & exercises that work, case studies that explain and insights & stories that explain all the "HOW's" and importantly, the "WHY's".

If business is a game of numbers, it helps to know the numbers that count!

"Fantastic workshop! Very easy to understand and such valuable and insightful information. A must for every business owner!"

Airlie Coleman, Base Bookkeeping

KNOW YOUR
NUMBERS
SPEAKER TOPIC 5

Imagine a small plane flying over the Pacific Ocean. Halfway across the captain announces, "I've got bad news and I've got good news."

The bad news is that the gauges aren't working. We are hopelessly lost, I have no idea how fast we are flying or in what direction, and I don't know how much fuel we have left.

The good news is that we are making great time!"

Does that sound at all familiar?

That's how most business owners run their numbers. They're flying blind with no dashboard to let them gauge where they are, where they are going, or if they are heading in the the right direction.

But somehow they always remain optimistic!

BECOME A
GOAL DIGGER
SPEAKER TOPIC 6

Your complete guide to running a business that exists for Good. The good of its founders, its clients, its team & the world.

Learn how join the growing global 'Business for Good' movement by aligning your business to the 17 UN Global Goals - becoming a 'GOAL DIGGER'.

They are a New WAY & and New WHY for business owners to both grow their business, their impact and their legacy.

Welcome to a new pathway for business - or maybe even a new pathway for humanity.

"We can't be the experts on everything but knowledge is powerful so listen to these guys (Ben & Harvee)"

Dr William Huynh, Be Well Dental

INSPIRE BEFORE YOU EXPIRE
SPEAKER TOPIC 7

They say, "the two most important days of your life are the day you are born, and the day you find out why". So what is your purpose?

See, our days are numbered ... We don't know when our time on this planet will be up.

What if, instead of leaving a legacy, we could LIVE our legacy now.

Learn the why, what & how of living a life on purpose, enabling you to INSPIRE BEFORE YOU EXPIRE.

Harvee Pene from Inspire CA - Life Changing Accountants. Thanks for empowering our kids & inspiring our young change makers at Business Camp in Brisbane. We all LOVE our Cashed Up Clap!

Taj Pabari, Young Australian of the Year

ACCOUNTANTS CHANGE LIVES!

SPEAKER TOPIC 8

Most business owners think that "ACCOUNTANTS ARE BORING."

Truth is, they have the power to help -

* Avoid cash flow crises
* Protect family assets
* Eliminate unnecessary business expenses
* Grow businesses by focusing on KPI's
* Get clarity and a sense of control & direction
* Think through a business model & direction
* Ensure a legacy through Estate Planning
* Ask the hard questions
* Automate invoicing processes.

In short, Accountants Change Lives.

This presentation suits conferences, lecture halls & events of Accounting Professionals, Accountants & Future Accountants.

GET PROFIT

8 HR PROFIT ACCELERATION WORKSHOP

You were put on this earth to do more than simply ... BREAK EVEN.

But if you want to make more profit and less loss, you need to -

1- Build a Profit War Chest.
2 - Know Your Numbers.
3 - Stop Giving Half Your Profits to the Tax Man.

Enjoy an inspiring day of mastering the 5 P's of Profit - Psychology, Priority, Predictability, Protections & Purpose.

"What a magic day with Harvee and Ben at Get Profit.♥ . The key framework these guys provide has been a missing piece in my business operations. Super grateful to come away with so much clarity for how to get cashed up so my business can do more good in the world. ☺"

Jaemin Frazer, The Insecurity Project

MORE MONEY, TIME & HAPPINESS

2 DAY BUSINESS & LIFESTYLE OPTIMISATION RETREAT

Over two days you will develop a series of 12 month plans, strategies and budgets to help you pull more money, time and happiness from your business.

These will become valuable assets that you will refer to on a daily or weekly basis to allow you to Boost Profits and Accelerate Cashflow in your business.

Based on implementation of the model in the Cashed Up book - 7 steps to pull more money, time & happiness from your business.

"I've never met such groovy, amazing and connected Accountants in my life!"

Phillip Di Bella. The original King of Coffee Culture

WEALTH FOR LIFE

2 DAY PERSONAL WEALTH & LIFESTYLE RETREAT

Let's turn your business profits into personal assets that will build your family legacy.

Most arguments in a marriage are around Money, and our mission is to reverse the statistics on divorce by getting couples on the same page about finances.

Focused around building true riches in all areas of wealth - Financial, Time, Physical & Relationships.

"Inspire CA takes the fear away from numbers and makes it real. They feel more like a business partner than just an Accountant."

Sharon Cliffe, Cider Consulting

BUSINESS FOR GOOD

2 DAY PURPOSE, PROFIT & PHILANTHROPY RETREAT

You've probably heard the adage - Businesses who do good, do better. Well this retreat will help you do better at doing good.

Over 1.5 inspiring days we will re-engineer your business to make super profits. This will be followed by a life-changing visit to a village to see first hand the impact that can be made when a business choses to use their profits for a higher purpose.

This is an international retreat hosted annually from 2020 in Bali, Vietnam & Cambodia.

"It's great to learn more about the bigger impact so many businesses are making thanks to the business for good movement. Every conversation has been incredibly inspiring."

Brandon Peart, Content Jet.

ACCOUNTANTS FOR GOOD

2 DAY PURPOSE, PROFIT & PHILANTHROPY RETREAT

for Accounting Firm Owners.

How can Accountants go from 'Boring' to 'Great' by doing more GOOD?

The UN Global Goals provides a NEW WAY & a NEW WHY for the Accounting Profession to grow their business and the impact they have on the world.

This retreat suits Accounting firm owners and will be run regularly in USA, UK & AU from 2020.

"Harvee shows a real generosity of spirit when sharing his time and he is truly insightful and knowledgeable in the areas of business improvement for today's professional practice."

Chris Beks. Ceebeks Accountants & Advisors

Topic 1
GOOD IS THE
NEW GREAT!

Topic 2
STOP **GIVING**
HALF YOUR PROFITS
TO THE TAX MAN!

Topic 3
BUILD YOUR
PROFIT WAR CHEST

Topic 4
GET **CASHED UP!**

Topic 5
KNOW **YOUR NUMBERS**

Topic 6
BECOME A
GOAL DIGGER

Topic 7
INSPIRE **BEFORE**
YOU EXPIRE

Topic 8
ACCOUNTANTS
CHANGE LIVES.

Workshop 1
GET PROFIT
8 HR Profit Workshop

Retreat 1
MORE MONEY, TIME
& HAPPINESS
2 Day Business Profit
& Lifestyle Retreat.

Retreat 2
WEALTH FOR LIFE
2 Day Personal Wealth
& Lifestyle Retreat

Retreat 3
BUSINESS FOR GOOD
2 Day Profit, Purpose &
Philanthropy Retreat
for Business Owners.

Retreat 4
ACCOUNTANTS FOR GOOD
2 Day Profit, Purpose &
Philanthropy Retreat
for Accounting Firm Owners.

Family.
Your most
important
business.

Harvee's Speaker Topic Summary - Inspiring Keynotes, Panel Discussions, Workshops & Retreats

Ben Murphy
Wellness Transformation
Specialist at Kula Health
August 14, 2019. Harvee was a
client of Ben's

HP, so authentic and such an inspiring speaker. A master communicator who we love connecting with!

Garry Millburn
Gladiator - Financial Coach
August 11, 2019. Harvee was a
client of Garry's

I have seen Harvee speak twice now. He delivers clear and concise thoughts that challenge the status quo! I truely believe in his efforts to make life more than just about the numbers. If you are looking for proactive and life changing accountants then Harvee and the Inspire are on your side!

Harold (Harry) Tsiamis
Specialising in the Design &
Installation of the Most
Intelligent Home Security &
Automation Systems for
Brisbane Homes
August 12, 2019. Harold (Harry)
worked with Harvee but at
different companies

I just wanted to take a quick moment to give a 'shout out' to Harvee, when I recently got to meet him and hear him present at a Key Person of Influence workshop in Brisbane

He's a true professional from beginning to end. If I were asked to pick a handful of words to describe him I immediately think of: friendly, accommodating, authentic, generous, professional, intuitive, and quick-witted.

The stand he takes for 'businesses being better by helping others' is humbling, and his presentation sharing his life journey was very in tune with the theme of the workshop.

He tailored a message that was spot on in the material, highly engaging and humorous in his delivery, and he held the audience's attention captive the entire time he was on stage!

After having the pleasure of experiencing Harvee present, I would highly and strongly recommend him for any future speaking event, because of the tremendous value he'll add. See less

Hunter Leonard
Author | Speaker | Mature
Age Advocate | Business
Owner
August 12, 2019. Harvee was a
client of Hunter's

Harvee is a rare, once in a generation kind of guy. He is not only a great business owner, but he speaks with passion and gratitude, and he really cares about leaving the planet a better place. He does this through action not words. I highly recommend you grab any chance to hear Harvee speak, and if you're looking for an inspirational person to add to your event as a keynote speaker, stop looking - you found your guy. See less

**Paul Dunn | The
Stunning Power of
Small**
🔆 B1G1 Chairman ● TEDx
Speaker ● Master Presenter
● Mentor Global
Entrepreneurs ● Host:
Global Impact Summit 🔆
August 13, 2019. Paul Dunn
worked with Harvee but at
different companies

The most frequent word I use when I'm speaking about Harvee Pene is this 'S T U N N I N G'.

When I see him speaking I am stunned by how authentic and connecting he is — no 'F-bombs' like so many people — just awesomely great insights time and time again, moving business and our world forward in superb ways.

And what makes those insights especially great is this: Harvee just doesn't talk about them — he does them and lives them each and every day.

He's a joy to be with. I feel privileged to know him.

And I'm willing to bet that you'll feel precisely the same way when you connect with him too. See less

David Cunningham
Business Excellence
Manager Southern
Queensland at ANZ
August 13, 2019. Harvee was a
client of David's

I have had the pleasure of hearing Harvee speak twice now. Not only is his message genuine and thought provoking but his ability to capture and engage the audience is masterful. I would recommend Harvee to anyone who wants to motivate their teams to do great things.

Joanne (Jo) Schonheim
CAO - Chief Accountability
Officer at Dent Global |
Relationship Builder |
Creative Thinker
August 13, 2019. Harvee was a
client of Joanne (Jo)'s

From the moment Harvee walks on stage, the audience can feel that they're in for a real treat. The energy that he brings, the authenticity with which he communicates, his generosity of spirit and his highly engaging manner, captivate the crowd instantly. He speaks from the heart, shares personal stories and insights, which make his content all the more impactful and critically relatable. Harvee leaves people enriched, enlightened, entertained and with a smile on their face that endures long past his presentation. He shifts the way people think. And he leaves them feeling excited and empowered, with an action plan of next steps to bring their ideas to life. See less

Carla Maree Simpson
Professional speaker,
Author and podcast host
August 16, 2019. Carla Maree
worked with Harvee but at
different companies

Harvee is a brilliant speaker, really helped and inspired me to take more control over my business and finances Cant wait to see him again Thanks Harvee

Taj Pabari
Teen Founder of Fiftysix
Creations - One for One
Entrepreneurship for Kids
August 12, 2016, Taj worked
with Harvee but at different
companies

Harvee was a rock star. His ability to deliver a motivating and educationally enriching message to a group of children in a funny, energetic and engaging way was incredible. His message was thought-provoking and resonated with the children for the entire event. We really enjoyed meeting and working with Harvee and we would love to have him come back to speak at future events! See less

Simon Banks - Keynote Speaker
Author | Creativity and
Innovation Expert | Keynote
Speaker | Conference
Emcee | Illustrator and Artist
August 16, 2019, Harvee was a
client of Simon Banks

I have been working in the conference and events industry for 20 years - Producing and Designing and MC'ing and Speaking and have seen some absolutely amazing speakers and storytellers. Harvee is one of them.
His stage presence and ability to draw you with great metaphors and stories is literally second to none. He makes the complex simple and his content sticks! One of his stories will be in my mind forever - with a big smile to go with it.
Most importantly, he is 100% authentic (and personable and funny as hell to boot).
I couldn't recommend Harvee highly enough.
Simon Banks

Ian Jacob
#1 HubSpot Focussed
Podcast in ANZ / APAC |
Marketing Automation |
Leads and Revenue Growth
Expert
August 18, 2019, Ian worked
with Harvee but in different
companies

From the first time I heard Harvee speak at a Dent community event, I have been impressed and blown away. He shares his story and passion so clearly, it makes everyone stand up and take note. I have had the privilege to hear him speak again at Dent & Inspire events and he does not fail! Keep up the great work of changing lives and businesses Harvee. See less

Jack O'Brien
Clinic Growth Team +
Leadership Marketing /
Client Attraction Client
Experiences Build a
#clinicforgood
August 14, 2019, Jack worked
with Harvee but at different
companies

I can recommend Harvee to the highest degree - he is simply incredible. As a speaker, Harvee is well spoken, inspiring, and easy to work with. Pre, during and post event, Harvee and his team were impeccable - they had materials and gifts for our delegates, their tech was prepared and adaptable, and there was no hard sell or bait and switch. The content was fresh and engaging, and the majority of our guests rated Harvee as their favourite speaker from the entire event! See less

Jaemin Frazer
TEDx Speaker | Author |
Founder of the Insecurity
Project | One of Australia's
leading life coaches
August 12, 2019, Harvee was a
client of Jaemin x

I've had the privilege of hearing Harvee deliver presentations twice. His content is world class and his delivery style is ultra engaging. He speaks freely out of the overflow of his own journey and is so authentic and passionate about what he offers. His rare mix of qualities and experience makes him unmissable as a speaker. See less

Anna Sheppard
The Corporate Kindness
Leadership Network
August 12, 2019, Harvee was a
client of Anna's

Harvee is such a warm and authentic speaker and one of the biggest areas of approval and feedback from our event attendees. He is a real Game Changer with a massive amount of knowledge in the business and accounting space. Such a great addition to our lineup of social entrepreneurs and business leaders. Harvee is a real authority and a must for any leadership conference, business strategy or thought leadership event. See less

Ale Wiecek
Human Centred Design
Strategist, Empathy Expert,
Keynote Speaker, Deepecho
Ian and Founder at Sur One
August 13, 2019, Harvee was a
client of Ale's

Harvee is a thought provoking and inspiring speaker, always so nimble, knowledge and purposely focus on leaving the audience with insights and new ways of creating impact in the world.

His calm and friendly manner resonates beautifully with his audience, leaving them want more.

I can't personally wait to hear Harvee again! See less

Carolyn Butler-Madden
Author | Speaker | Social
Purpose & Cause Marketing
Specialist
August 12, 2019, Harvee was a
client of Carolyn's

I've had the pleasure of seeing Harvee Pene speak on a number of occasions. Three different events. Two of those events to an entrepreneurial small business audience (a B1G1 conference and a Dent Conference). The third time I saw him speak was at Bambuddha's Corporate Kindness event, a mixed audience of non-profit, corporate, social enterprise and SME's.

It is testament to his personal style that Harvee can connect so well with his audience across such a broad reach.

Harvee is a storyteller and someone who inspires. He's quietly spoken but his message rings out with powerful resonance. He'll make your audience laugh and he'll make them cry.

If you want someone who can inspire your audience by direct example, that doing good is good for business, Harvee's your man. See less

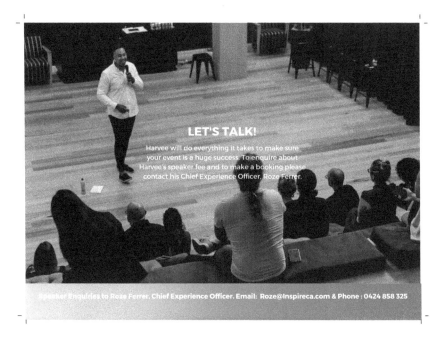

LET'S TALK!

Harvee will do everything it takes to make sure your event is a huge success. To enquire about Harvee's speaker fee and to make a booking please contact his Chief Experience Officer, Roze Ferrer.

Speaker Enquiries to Roze Ferrer. Chief Experience Officer. Email: Roze@Inspireca.com & Phone : 0424 858 325

Lightning Source UK Ltd.
Milton Keynes UK
UKHW022136110722
405708UK00006B/206

9 780645 236774